THE CATHOLIC BISHOPS AND THE ECONOMY
A Debate

SOCIAL
PHILOSOPHY
& POLICY CENTER

THE CATHOLIC BISHOPS AND THE ECONOMY
A Debate

Douglas Rasmussen
and
James Sterba

Transaction Books
New Brunswick (USA) and London (UK)

BX
1795
, E27
c37
1987
suppl.2

Published by the Social Philosophy and Policy Center
and by Transaction, Inc. 1987

Copyright © by the Social Philosophy and Policy Center

Library of Congress Cataloging-in-Publication Data

Rasmussen, Douglas B., 1948-
    The Catholic bishops and the economy.

    (Studies in social philosophy & policy; no. 9)
    Includes bibliographies.
    1. Catholic Church. National Conference of Catholic
Bishops. Pastoral Letter on Catholic social teaching and
the U.S. economic.   2. Economics — Religious aspects —
Catholic Church.   3. Sociology, Christian (Catholic)
4. United States — Economic conditions — 1981-
I. Sterba, James P.   II. Title.   III. Series.
BX1795.E27C37   1986 Suppl. 2   261.85   86-27269
ISBN 0-912051-15-9
ISBN 0-912051-16-7 (pbk.)

Cover Design: Jacky Ahrens

TABLE OF CONTENTS

Introduction

When the National Conference of Catholic Bishops published the first draft of their pastoral letter on the U.S. economy in November 1984, it generated a storm of controversy that has yet to abate. Supporters and detractors alike recognized immediately that it would play an important role in the public debate on economic policy in the United States. The third and final draft of the pastoral, entitled *Economic Justice for All: Catholic Social Teaching and the U.S.Economy,*[1] is the result of two years spent revising and refining the original document. The bishops have considered responses and comments from all across the political and religious spectrum in preparing this final statement, and it promises to be no less important than the original.

In this volume, two highly regarded philosophers steeped in the Catholic tradition examine the *Economic Pastoral.* One provides additional philosophical support for the bishops' position, while the other disputes the bishops' policy prescriptions. Previous discussions of the *Economic Pastoral* have generally addressed either the Biblical foundation that the bishops claim for their position or the practicality of the bishops' policy prescriptions. The essays in this volume make a new contribution to the debate, in that they consider the question of whether or not the bishops' views can be justified in philosophical terms.

The bishops' motivation for writing the *Economic Pastoral* is the host of economic problems that plagues the United States and the world. Poverty, unemployment, the erosion of stable family structures, massive expenditures on weapons, and so forth, are problems that threaten the dignity and well-being of people throughout the world. And, the bishops claim, they are problems that can only be solved through the collective efforts of all concerned human beings. Thus, the bishops seek to bring about a new spirit of cooperation and a new vision of what the ideal of economic justice requires of us all. In their own words, they write not only to provide guidance for the members of their own church, but also to elicit "the cooperation and support of those who do not share our faith or tradition.

The common bond of humanity that links all persons is the source of our belief that the country can attain a renewed public moral vision."[2]

The source of this renewed moral vision is the Biblical message that there is "a God who is creator of heaven and earth, and of the human family" and that human beings stand at the summit of creation.[3] This leads the bishops to reflect on our special relationship to God and the rest of His creation:

> The biblical vision of creation has provided one of the most enduring legacies of church teaching. To stand before God as creator is to respect God's creation, both the world of nature and of human history. *From the patristic period to the present, the church has affirmed that misuse of the world's resources or appropriation of them by a minority of the world's population betrays the gift of creation since "whatever belongs to God belongs to all."*[4]

The bishops draw on this tradition of church teaching to articulate a vision of individual and social well-being that they hope can guide us through the intricate economic problems of the modern world.

The core of this renewed moral vision is a conception of human dignity. "The fundamental moral criterion for all economic decisions, policies and institutions is this: They must be at the service of *all people, especially the poor*....[H]uman dignity, realized in community with others and with the whole of God's creation, is the norm against which every social institution must be measured."[5] In Catholic social thought, human dignity is not only a right of the individual, but a right of the community as well. It "can only be realized and protected in solidarity with others" in communities which "allow social groups and their individual members relatively thorough and ready access to their own fulfillment."[6] Thus, social institutions must be constructed in such a way as to ensure that individuals have access to material goods and are secure in the fundamental freedoms and interpersonal relationships that are indispensable for participation in social life. If the economy is to nourish and protect human dignity, it must, at a minimum, secure for each individual the rights to food, clothing, shelter, medical care, and basic education. The denial of any of these rights harms the individual and thereby injures the community as well.

This conception of the relationship between human dignity and social life is captured in the norms of basic justice. The bishops distinguish three dimensions of basic justice. First, commutative justice dictates *"fundamental fairness in all agreements and exchanges between individuals or private social groups....*For example, workers owe their employers diligent work in exchange for their wages. Employers are obligated to treat their employees as persons, paying them fair wages in exchange for the work done and establishing conditions and patterns of work that are truly human."[7] Second, distributive justice requires "*that the allocation of income, wealth and power in society be evaluated in light of its effects on persons whose basic material needs are unmet.*"[8] When resources are sufficient to the task, as they certainly are in the United States today, the community must fulfill the basic needs of all. Third, social justice entails "*that persons have an obligation to be active and productive participants in the life of society and that society has a duty to enable them to participate in this way.*"[9] The requirements of justice are, thus, that we secure to every human being well-being and dignity by promoting the conditions of social life that make such a life possible.

> Basic justice...calls for the establishment of a floor of material well-being on which all can stand. This is a duty of the whole of society, and it creates particular obligations for those with greater resources. This duty calls into question extreme inequalities of income and consumption when so many lack basic necessities. Catholic social teaching does not maintain that a flat, arithmetical equality of income and wealth is a demand of justice, but it does challenge economic arrangements that leave large numbers of people impoverished. Further, it sees extreme inequality as a threat to the solidarity of the human community, for great disparities lead to deep social divisions and conflict.[10]

This is the renewed moral vision that the bishops hope will fire the spirit of cooperation and commitment that is needed to meet the economic problems that face this country and the world.

Much of the controversy surrounding the *Economic Pastoral* has focused on the bishops' application of this moral vision to specific economic issues. The bishops recognize that issues of policy are subject to differing interpretations and do not claim the same moral authority for their policy recommendations as for their statements of moral principles. However, they nonetheless think it worthwhile to illustrate their moral principles with specific applications. They do so by considering four economic issues.

(1) Employment

The basic right to employment guarantees that the individual can participate in the economic life of society. Through employment, persons attain self-realization and provide the essential material goods necessary for their sustenance: "[H]uman work has a special dignity and is a key to achieving justice in society."[11] As a nation, the bishops believe, we have an obligation to make it possible for all who seek employment to find it. But the bishops cite studies which indicate that the level of unemployment has been steadily increasing in recent years. Joblessness is a problem that is deeply entrenched in our society.

Unemployment affects both the individual and society. The individual's sense of self-worth is eroded: there is no productive role for this person to fill in society. Every day he remains unemployed, society seems to say: Who needs your talent? Who needs your initiative? Who needs *you*? Society itself is harmed because the unemployed person pays few, if any, taxes, thereby lowering tax revenues to all levels of government; society makes greater expenditures for unemployment compensation, food stamps, and welfare; and crime increases. "[A]s a nation we simply cannot afford to have millions of able-bodied men and women unemployed."[12]

The problem of joblessness is exacerbated by several factors, according to the bishops. Population growth, spurred by the post-World War II baby boom, has increased the pool of prospective employees. Women also are entering the work force in greater numbers than ever before. And immigrants seeking their own version of the American dream enlarge the labor force. The number of available jobs has also decreased, they contend: advancing technology displaces the human workman, and increasing competition in world markets reduces the need for U.S. products and leads some U.S. companies to move to foreign lands where wages are lower. High defense spending also contributes to the loss of jobs, since "defense industries are less labor-intensive than other major sectors of the economy."[13]

The bishops suggest a general plan of action to combat the blight of unemployment. We must agree that each person has a right to employment and promote the type of public policy that can make full employment a reality: "*the fiscal and monetary policies of the nation—such as federal spending, tax and interest-rate policies—should be coordinated*"[14] to achieve this end, and inflation must be checked by effective new policies. More specifically, the *Economic Pastoral* calls for the expansion of job-training and apprenticeship programs which will develop the technical and professional skills needed by our advancing society. It also recommends "*increased support for direct job-creation progams targeted on the long-term unemployed and those with special needs.*"[15] Such job-generation programs would be targeted at those with inadequate job skills who have the most difficulty in breaking out of the unemployment cycle. Other strategies recommended by the bishops include greater job sharing, more use of flex time, a reduction in the length of the workweek, a limitation or elimination of overtime, an end to the overuse of part-time employees, and improved job placement services.

(2) Poverty

According to official government standards, about one in every seven Americans lives in poverty today. And while there are flaws in government statistics on poverty, one fact is clear to the bishops: a significant number of Americans lack the resources necessary to lead a decent life. This fact is especially alarming to them in view of the uneven distribution of wealth and income that marks the U.S. economy. They cite statistics which show that 57 percent of the country's net wealth is held by the richest 10 percent of families; when homes and other real estate are excluded, this figure rises to 86 percent. Absolute equality in the distribution of income and wealth is not the goal of Catholic social teaching. But this unequal distribution underscores "the priority of meeting the basic needs of the poor and the importance of increasing the level of participation by all members of society,"[16] for a natural consequence of the uneven distribution of wealth is the unequal distribution of political and social power.

The bishops propose extensive measures for combatting poverty. First and foremost, we must build a healthy economy which provides full employment. Beyond this, the impoverished must be given the power to take control of their own lives: "Paternalistic programs which do too much *for* and too little *with* the poor are to be avoided."[17] More specifically, employment at just and equal wages must be made available for all able-bodied adults; self-help projects, such as low-income housing and worker cooperatives, should be emphasized; the tax system should be reformed, so that those below the official poverty level pay no (or minimal) taxes; and education for the poor must be improved. Additionally, the family unit itself must be strengthened because single-parent families headed by women are disproportionately represented among the ranks of the poor. Thus, there is a pressing need for better child-care services and job security for parents who want to spend time at home with a new baby, and for programs to decrease the high rates of divorce and teenage pregnancy.

The *Economic Pastoral* also calls for a thorough reform of the nation's welfare system. The bishops suggest four particular improvements that are needed. First, when a welfare recipient seizes the opportunity to enter gainful employment, he should not be made worse off than he was when he relied on public assistance. Currently, the bishops point out, those who leave the welfare rolls soon lose Medicaid benefits, no matter what their new salary is. Second, a welfare recipient should not have to survive on public assistance which does not elevate him above the poverty level. Welfare must provide adequate levels of support. Third, benefit levels and eligibility criteria of public assistance programs should be standardized nationally. These factors currently vary dramatically among states. And fourth, needy two-parent families should receive public assistance just as single-parent families do. The unemployed or low-paid father should not have to leave his family in order for the family to receive aid.

(3) Food and Agriculture

In the early history of the United States farm system, the small farm worked by its owner-operator was the norm. But recent years have seen the emergence of a trend toward the farming conglomerate run by professional managers. The economic woes of the small owner-operator have brought this about. During the 1970s, new markets for exporting farm goods opened. Perceiving the opportunity for increased profits, the small farmer secured bank loans which provided the capital needed to industrialize the farm and thus make it more productive and more profitable. The 1980s, however, brought shrinking export markets and declines in commodity prices and land values. The result, according to the bishops, has been bankruptcy for many small farmers and the emergence of larger, more capital-intensive (and environmentally unsound) farming operations.

The *Economic Pastoral* calls for a three-pronged approach to these problems. First, the owner-operated farm must be preserved. The owner-operator is responsive to public need, because he is part of the public served by the farmer. He also helps to stabilize food markets, since the consumer need not depend on business decisions made by the farming conglomerate seeking to maximize the return on its investment. Second, farming is to be protected as valuable work. Unemployment is already high, and a bankrupt farm will mean not only the loss of work for the farmer and those in his immediate employ, but also the loss of jobs in other rural businesses. Third, U.S. agriculture must use natural resources in ways that do not damage or deplete them.

The bishops urge government action to ensure that family farms have access to emergency credit and low-interest loans, and the rural lending institutions where farm loans are held should also have temporary assistance available to them. Federal farm programs which disproportionately benefit large farms should be reapportioned to better aid the small farmer. Tax policies which provide tax shelters in large farms should also be reformed. Research efforts by government and universities should be redirected to improving small farm productivity. Government should also encourage farm conservation measures and guarantee minimum wages and benefits for farmhands.

Finally, the pastoral makes a plea to farmers: "The ever-present tempta-
tion to individualism and greed must be countered by a determined movement toward solidarity....It is not necessary for every farmer to be in
competition against every other farmer."[18]

(4) The Role of the United States in the Global Economy

Fourth and last among the economic issues the bishops discuss is the
United States' role in the world economy. Because the U.S. is such a domi-
nant force in international affairs, developing countries often perceive
themselves as dependent on us. The bishops believe that because this per-
ception of dependence is so often a result of our own policies, the United
States should "promote public policies that increase the ability of poor
nations and marginalized people to participate in the global economy."[19]
Human dignity and economic development must no longer take second
place to political and strategic concerns in our foreign policy. The bishops
list five specific ways in which we can improve our foreign policy. First, the
U.S. should increase foreign aid in proportion to the gross national product. Second, an equitable system of trade must be established which will
ensure that Third World countries receive fair prices for their exported
goods. Third, the debtor-creditor relationship between countries must be
altered by reducing or cancelling debts. Fourth, direct foreign investment
should be encouraged, for it provides the capital, technology, and man-
agerial expertise that the developing countries so desperately need. And
fifth, changes must be made in the international food production and
distribution system. The U.S. must cooperate in increasing food aid and
establishing long-term programs which will teach the food-deficient developing countries self-reliance.

The essays that comprise this volume examine both the philosophical
foundations of the bishops' "renewed moral vision" and their proposals for
how to make this vision a reality. The format of the volume is that of a
debate: each author makes an extended opening statement in which he
offers a critical assessment of the bishops' arguments; these opening statements are followed by rejoinders in which the authors address one another
directly. The authors come to this discussion from backgrounds that include significant scholarship in political philosophy and the Catholic philosophical tradition. James Sterba is Professor of Philosophy at the
University of Notre Dame. He has published extensively on ethical and
political theory and on such policy issues as abortion, nuclear weapons,
and welfare, and he has presented papers on such topics to the American
Catholic Philosophical Association. Douglas Rasmussen is Associate Pro-

fessor of Philosophy at St. John's University. He has published on Aristotelian philosophy and the theory of human rights, and has served on the faculties of a number of Catholic colleges and universities. Both are steeped in the tradition of Catholic social teaching, as well as the intricacies of modern political philosophy.

Professor Sterba defends the *Economic Pastoral* against critics who claim that its policy proposals are not well conceived. He argues that they are exactly the sorts of policies we must adopt if we are genuinely concerned with human freedom and well-being. Sterba grounds this conclusion on an analysis of three competing conceptions of human dignity, which he terms *libertarian, socialist,* and *welfare liberal.* These are, Sterba argues, the primary conceptions of human dignity that are found in contemporary political theory. And while they differ radically in theoretical terms, he maintains, they have essentially the same implications for public policy: all three conceptions of human dignity support the kinds of policies recommended by the bishops in the *Economic Pastoral.*

Professor Rasmussen, although he shares the bishops' concern for human dignity, argues that their policy proposals are based on an inadequate and flawed understanding of this notion. The bishops have, he maintains, failed to see the important role that autonomy—self-directed action in pursuit of one's own, freely chosen goals—plays in the realization of the ideal of a life of dignity for every individual. According to Rasmussen, autonomy is not simply one of the components of a life of dignity, neither more nor less important than meaningful work or education. It is, rather, the very essence of human dignity, for it is the capacity to act autonomously that distinguishes human beings from other natural creatures. Rasmussen contends that many of the policies advocated by the bishops undermine autonomy: insofar as they make it a requirement of law that we give aid to those in need and that governments guarantee the well-being of all, they deprive us of the responsibility to choose for ourselves how we shall live.

The application of moral principles to the pressing economic problems of the day is a matter of fundamental importance. The issues raised by the *Economic Pastoral* and addressed by Sterba and Rasmussen are central to an understanding of how we may best protect the dignity and well-being of individuals in the United States and throughout the world. These are complex issues, and the task of enhancing human dignity is a difficult one. It is hoped that these essays will make a significant contribution to the ongoing debate on the *Economic Pastoral.*

PART 1

The Bishops' Letter on the U.S. Economy: A Philosophical Defense

James Sterba

Everyone who has publicly commented on the *Pastoral Letter on Catholic Social Teaching and the U.S. Economy* would agree, I think, that the letter is an important document.[1] Opponents as well as supporters of the *Economic Pastoral* would concur in this assessment, especially now that the document has been overwhelmingly endorsed by the U.S. Catholic Bishops, because it is likely that many people, especially Catholics, will come to accept or at least seriously consider its conclusions. Supporters of the *Economic Pastoral*, however, also think that the letter is an important document because many or most of its conclusions are morally sound. As a supporter of the *Economic Pastoral*, I think that it has this twofold importance. At the same time, I think that the conclusions of the *Economic Pastoral*, while morally sound, are not adequately justified from a philosophical point of view. In what follows, I propose to provide this missing philosophical defense. To adequately set the stage for this defense, I will begin by briefly summarizing the *Economic Pastoral*. I will then review the major criticisms that have been directed against the letter and consider what responses might be made to these criticisms before turning to my own philosophical defense.

I. The Economic Pastoral: A Summary

The *Economic Pastoral* begins with an account of the "signs of the times." These signs, which include high unemployment, increasing relative poverty and financial crisis among farmers in the U.S., and significant absolute poverty in developing and underdeveloped nations of the world, call for a moral response on our part. In their response, the U.S. Catholic

Bishops sought to apply Catholic social teaching to the U.S. Economy. The *Economic Pastoral* is the result.

The methodology of the letter, as Archbishop Weakland, who chaired the committee that drafted the letter, has emphasized, is basically deductive: Chapter 2 of the letter sets forth the principles from which the policy recommendations of later chapters are said to be deduced.[2] Now the ultimate principle set forth in Chapter 2 is said to have both a religious and a secular, or strictly philosophical, grounding. The proclaimed religious grounding derives from the Bible and from the post-Biblical tradition of the church, especially from modern Catholic thought "developed over the past century by the popes and the Second Vatican Council in response to modern economic conditions."[3] The proclaimed secular, or strictly philosophical grounding, derives from "the common bond of humanity that links all persons."[4]

The ultimate principle of Chapter 2 of the *Economic Pastoral* is:

> *The Principle of Human Dignity*
> The dignity of the human person realized in community with others is the criterion against which all aspects of economic life must be measured.[5]

This principle is said to give rise to "the responsibilities of social living,"[6] in particular, a duty to love one's neighbor and a duty to abide by the demands of justice.

The demands of justice according to the letter, are of these types:

(1) *Commutative justice*, which calls for fundamental fairness in all agreements and exchanges between individuals or private social groups.

(2) *Distributive justice*, which requires that the allocation of income, wealth, and power in society be evaluated in light of its effects on persons whose basic material needs are unmet.

(3) *Social justice*, which implies that persons have an obligation to be active and productive participants in the life of society and that society has a duty to enable them to participate in this way.

More specifically, the demands of justice are said to require:

(1) rights to life, food, clothing, shelter, rest, medical care, and basic education, which support a right to security in the event of sickness, unemployment, and old age;

(2) rights to employment, healthful working conditions, wages, and other benefits sufficient to provide individuals and their families with a standard of living in keeping with human dignity and the possibility of property ownership.

Taken together, the *Principle of Human Dignity* and its derived duties and rights are said to entail to a preferential "option for the poor"[7] requiring the following priorities:

(1) the fulfillment of the basic needs of the poor;

(2) increased active participation in economic life by those presently excluded or vulnerable;

(3) the investment of wealth, talent, and human energy that is especially directed to benefit those who are poor or economically insecure;

(4) economic and social policies and a mode of organization in the work world that strengthen and contribute to the stability of family life.

In sum, the Economic Pastoral calls for a new "American Experiment" in securing economic rights that guarantee the minimum conditions of human dignity for each and every person, paralleling the experiment in securing civil and political rights for each and every person launched by the founders of our country.

Applying the *Principle of Human Dignity* and its derived rights, duties and priorities to the U.S. Economy, the bishops are lead to endorse the following policy recommendations.

Employment

Fiscal and monetary policies of the nation should be coordinated in such a way that full employment is the primary goal. To achieve this goal, there should be an expansion of job-training and apprenticeship programs in the private sector which are jointly administered and supported by business, labor unions, and government, and there should be support for direct job-creation programs targeted at the structurally unemployed and those with special needs.

Poverty

A key element in removing poverty is prevention through a healthy economy. Nevertheless, vigorous action should be undertaken to remove barriers to full and equal employment for women and minorities. In addition, self-help efforts among the poor should be fostered by programs and policies in both the private and public sectors. Specifically, there is a need for reforms in the tax system that would reduce the burden on the poor, a much stronger commitment to education for the poor, and policies and programs at all levels to support the strength and stability of families, especially those adversely affected by the economy.

Welfare

A thorough reform of the nation's welfare and income-support programs should be undertaken so that welfare recipients are provided with adequate levels of support and also assisted, wherever possible, to become self-sufficient through gainful employment. In addition, there should be national eligibility standards and a national minimum benefit level for public assistance programs. Welfare programs should also be made available to two-parent as well as single-parent families.

Food and Agriculture

The economic viability of moderate-sized farms operated by families on a full-time basis should be preserved, and the opportunity to engage in farming should be protected as a valuable form of work. Moreover, effective stewardship of our natural resources should be a central consideration in any measures regarding U.S. agriculture.

United States and World Economy

U.S.–developing world relations should be determined in the first place by a concern for basic human needs and respect for cultural traditions. This requires a U.S. international economic policy that is designed to help empower people everywhere and give them a sense of their own worth, to help them improve the quality of their lives, and to ensure that the benefits of economic growth are shared equitably among them. In particular, rather than promoting U.S. arms sales, especially to countries that cannot afford them, we should be campaigning for an international agreement to restrict this lethal practice.

Economic Cooperation

In an advanced industrial economy like ours, all parts of society, including government, must cooperate in forming national economic policies; and in judging the moral status of these policies, the primary concern should be their impact on the poor and the vulnerable. This means that the serious distortion of national economic priorities produced by massive national spending on defense must be remedied.

The Church as Economic Agent

All the moral principles that govern the just operation of any economic endeavor apply to the church and its many agencies and institutions; indeed, the church should be exemplary.

The *Economic Pastoral* concludes by asking each one of us to consider to what degree the Biblical and ethical vision outlined in the letter has permeated our own thinking and our own way of life.

II. The Bishops and Public Policy

While admirers of the *Economic Pastoral* have found much to praise in the letter, critics of the letter, focusing mainly on what has become Chapter 3, have raised various objections to the policy recommendations contained in it. For example, Charles Krauthammer, an associate editor of *New Republic*, finds some of the letter's recommendations to be empty truisms. He writes:

> It simply won't do imperiously to proclaim that welfare programs "should encourage rather than penalize gainful employment." Of course, they should. But exactly how?

And when the bishops urge that "employment programs that generate jobs efficiently without entailing large expense and increased inflation should be emphasized," Krauthammer comments:

> Why, even Jesse Helms would welcome a noninflationary employment policy. The interesting question, to use scientific parlance, is exactly what that policy would be.[8]

Fortunately for the bishops, this line of criticism is not very damaging, since few of their policy recommendations are of this sort. Most of the letter's recommendations have their well-known opponents. For example, national eligibility standards and a national minimum benefit level for welfare, along with a reduction of the military budget and international arms sales, are clearly not priorities of the current Republican administration.

Probably with such opponents in mind, other critics have challenged the feasibility of the *Economic Pastoral's* policy recommendations. Thomas Reese, an associate editor of *America*, suggests that the bishops should "admit that, granted current economic conditions (the huge Federal deficit and the large military budget) its recommendations are not practical at this time."[9] Likewise, Governor Cuomo of New York finds the letter's call for national eligibility standards and a national minimum benefit level for public assistance programs to be a praiseworthy ideal but not feasible at the present moment.[10] However, as Archbishop Weakland has noted, whether something is or is not feasible given certain constraints is a morally relevant consideration only if the constraints themselves are morally acceptable.[11] And at least one constraint that is frequently cited in this context, namely, the large U.S. military budget, is certainly not considered by the bishops to be morally acceptable. As the bishops see it, the issue is "not whether the United States can provide the necessary funds to meet our social needs, but whether we have the political will to do so."[12]

Others have charged that the bishops are supporting policy recommendations that are essentially contestable and that, as a result, reasonable people could just as well support other policy recommendations. For example, Joseph Califano, who was special assistant for domestic affairs to President Johnson and Secretary of Health, Education and Welfare under President Carter, points out that while the *Economic Pastoral* recommends annual adjustment of welfare benefits to reflect increases in the cost of living, Johnson rigorously opposed automatic cost of living adjustments for social security and other government income maintenance programs on the ground that it forces recipients to put more pressure on Congress to fight inflation. Finding Johnson's policy to be at least as reasonable as the one the bishops propose, Califano criticizes the bishops for not avoiding policy recommendations that are essentially contestable.[13] In a similar vein, Andrew Greeley, an associate of the National Opinion Research Center in Chicago, contends that the bishops should not be endorsing a progressive tax policy when certain flat tax policies appear to be equally reasonable.[14] Yet without attempting to judge the reasonableness of these alternative policies, it is important to recognize that the bishops do not deny that at least some of their policy recommendations are essentially contestable and that, consequently, alternative recommendations could also be reasonable. As they put it:

> Our judgements and recommendations on specific economic issues, therefore, do not carry the same moral authority as our statements of universal moral principles and formal Church teaching; the former are related to circumstances which can change or which can be interpreted differently by people of good will.[15]

So the bishops are not trying to show that disagreement with their policy recommendations is in all cases unreasonable and immoral; critics who assume that they are are simply misinterpreting them. Nevertheless, while the bishops grant that there can be "diversity of opinion in the church and in U.S. society on how to protect human dignity and economic rights of all our brothers and sisters," they also maintain that "there can be no legitimate disagreement on the basic moral objectives."[16]

By far the most serious criticism that has been raised to the *Economic Pastoral* is that many of its recommendations simply endorse or extend Great Society programs that have failed. For example, Greeley writes:

> ...the bishops categorically endorse existing welfare programs and call for an increase in them, with no hint that they are aware that many liberals and neoliberals have lost confidence in the welfare approach to poverty. Need I say that this loss of confidence is not based on the assumption that society need do nothing about the poor? Rather, it is based on the growing conviction that most of what can broadly be called welfare, especially programs introduced since 1967, does not work and indeed does more harm than good.[17]

Obviously this wide-ranging criticism requires an equally wide-ranging response. In the second draft of the letter, the bishops thought it appropriate to include just such a response:

> Our history shows that we can reduce poverty. During the 1960s and early 1970s the official poverty rate was cut in half, due not only to a healthy economy but also to public-policy decisions that improved the nation's income-transfer programs. It is estimated, for example, that in the late 1970s federal benefit programs were lifting out of poverty about 70 percent of those who would have otherwise been poor.

> During the last 25 years the Social Security program has dramatically reduced poverty among the elderly. In addition, in 1983 it lifted out of poverty almost 1.5 million children of retired, deceased and disabled workers. Medicare has enhanced the life expectancy and health status of elderly and disabled people, and Medicaid has reduced infant mortality and greatly improved access to health care for the poor.[18]

This criticism of the *Economic Pastoral* and the bishops' response parallels the public discussion evoked by Charles Murray's book, *Losing Ground.* In that book, Murray summarizes his central argument as follows:

> Basic indicators of well-being took a turn for the worse in the 1960s, most consistently and most drastically for the poor. In some cases, earlier progress slowed; in other cases mild deterioration accelerated; in a few instances advance turned into retreat. The trendlines on many of the indicators are—literally—unbelievable to people who do not make a profession of following them.

The question is why. Why at that moment in the history did so many basic trends in the quality of life *for the poor* go sour? Why did progress slow, stop, reverse?

The easy hypotheses—the economy, changes in demographics, the effects of Vietnam or Watergate or racism—fail as explanations. As often as not, taking them into account only increases the mystery.

Nor does the explanation lie in idiosyncratic failures of craft. It is not just that we sometimes administered good programs improperly, or that sound concepts sometimes were converted to operations incorrectly. It is not that a specific program, or a specific court ruling or act of Congress, was especially destructive. The error was strategic.

A government's social policy helps set the rules of the game—the stakes, the risks, the payoffs, the tradeoffs, and the strategies for making a living, raising a family, having fun, defining what "winning" and "success" mean. The more vulnerable a population and the fewer its independent resources, the more decisive is the effect of the rules imposed from above. The most compelling explanation for the marked shift in the fortunes of the poor is that they continued to respond, as they always had, to the world as they found it but that we—meaning the not-poor and un-disadvantaged—had changed the rules of their world. Not of our world, just of theirs. The first effect of the new rules was to make it profitable for the poor to behave in the short term in ways that were destructive in the long term. Their second effect was to mask these long-term losses—to subsidize irretrievable mistakes. We tried to provide more for the poor and produced more poor instead. We tried to remove the barriers to escape from poverty, and inadvertently built a trap.[19]

Yet while Murray's book has been widely hailed in certain quarters, critics have argued that the relevant data do not support his argument. For example, Michael Harrington, who is co-chair of Democratic Socialists of America, points out that while black male labor force participation did drop 7 percent between 1969-1981 (thus fitting nicely with Murray's thesis that welfare programs are the villain) there was a drop of 7.4 percent between 1955 and 1968.[20] So the drop in employment was actually greater before welfare programs came on line than it was after, just the opposite of what Murray's thesis would lead us to expect.

Or consider black women. Supposedly, they are even more exposed than men to the supposed work disincentives of welfare programs since as mothers they can qualify for Aid to Families of Dependent Children. But as Harrington shows, their labor force participation rate increased between 1955 and 1981 by 7.5 percent, and more than half of that progress occurred after 1968.

And on the question of whether welfare programs did any good, Christopher Jencks, who is a professor of Sociology and Urban Affairs at Northwestern University, claims that the relevant data tell a story that is quite different from the one Murray tells in *Losing Ground.* He writes:

> First, contrary to what Murray claims, "net" poverty declined almost as fast after 1965 as it had before. Second, the decline in poverty after 1965, unlike the decline before 1965, occurred despite unfavorable economic conditions, and depended to a great extent on government efforts to help the poor. Third, the groups that benefitted from this "generous revolution," as Murray rightly calls it, were precisely the groups that legislators hoped would benefit, notably the aged and the disabled. The groups that did not benefit were the ones that legislators did not especially want to help. Fourth, these improvements took place despite demographic changes that would ordinarily have made things worse. Given the difficulties, legislators should, I think, look back on their efforts to improve the material conditions of poor people's lives with some pride.[21]

Thus, it would appear that the relevant data not only fail to support Murray's argument, but also, *assuming the validity of the principles endorsed by the Economic Pastoral,* provides adequate grounds for the bishops' commitment to the welfare programs of the Great Society.

Of course, I do not mean to suggest that the specific ways that the bishops propose to extend Great Society programs cannot be subject to criticism. Rather, all that has been shown is that the association of the bishops' practical recommendations with the Great Society programs cannot be used as a basis for criticizing them.

III. A Philosophical Defense of the Economic Pastoral

Yet even if the criticisms of the policy recommendations of the *Economic Pastoral* can be answered in the ways that have been suggested, there still remains a fundamental problem for the *Economic Pastoral.* The problem concerns the proclaimed deduction of the policy recommendations from the *Principle of Human Dignity* of Chapter 2. Now I think that when the *Principle of Human Dignity* is interpreted in the light of the Bible and the post-Biblical tradition of the church, the principle clearly favors most of the policy recommendations of the *Economic Pastoral.*[22] But the fundamental problem, as I see it, is that no such claim can be made when the principle is interpreted in a secular or strictly philosophical fashion. This is because there are alternative conceptions of human dignity that, at least at first glance, do not appear to require the set of economic rights and priorities endorsed by the bishops. More precisely, there are conceptions of human dignity that appear to require both less and more than what the bishops endorse.

Simplifying a bit, there appear to be three basic conceptions of human dignity. First, there is a libertarian conception of human dignity. In the last presidential election in the United States, David Bergland was the candidate whose views were closest to a libertarian conception of human dignity. But the candidate whose views were next closest, Ronald Reagan, was re-elected and continues to refashion the U.S. economy. Now, according to this conception of human dignity, liberty is the ultimate political ideal. Thus, all assignments of rights and duties are ultimately to be justified in terms of an ideal of liberty.

Second, there is a socialist conception of human dignity. In the United States there has never been a viable socialist presidential candidate, but elsewhere there have been many successful socialist candidates. Currently, Francois Mitterrand, a socialist, is president of France and Andreas Papandreou's Socialist Movement controls Greece's parliament. Now according to a socialist conception of human dignity, equality is the ultimate political ideal. Thus, all assignments of rights and duties are ultimately to be justified in terms of an ideal equality.

Third, there is a welfare liberal conception of human dignity. This is the conception endorsed, for example, by the left wing of the Democratic Party in the United States, whose leaders are Ted Kennedy, Jesse Jackson, and George McGovern. According to this conception, the ultimate political ideal is a blend of liberty and equality, and this blend, as we shall see, can be characterized as fairness or, more specifically, as contractual fairness. Thus, all assignments of rights and duties are ultimately to be justified in terms of an ideal of contractual fairness.[23]

So we have three conceptions of human dignity: a liberation conception which takes liberty to be the ultimate political ideal, a socialist conception which takes equality to be the ultimate political ideal, and a welfare liberal conception which takes a blend of liberty and equality, which can be characterized as contractual fairness, to be the ultimate political ideal. And it seems to me that, while there are other conceptions of human dignity, they all can be subsumed under one or another of these three main conceptions.[24] To defend philosophically the conclusions of the *Economic Pastoral*, therefore, it should suffice to show that each of these three conceptions of human dignity, when properly interpreted, in fact supports those same conclusions. Thus, I propose to show that whether people are committed to a libertarian conception of human dignity which takes liberty to be the ultimate political ideal, or to a socialist conception of human dignity which takes equality to be the ultimate political ideal, or to a welfare liberal conception of human dignity which takes a blend of liberty and equality to be the ultimate political ideal, they all should support the conclusions of the *Economic Pastoral.*

I want to begin by focusing on the distribution in our society of two items which are at the heart of the *Economic Pastoral's* policy recommendations: welfare checks and affirmative action acceptance letters. Welfare checks, let us suppose, are distributed only to those who are unable to work or for the support of dependent children. Affirmative action acceptance letters, let us suppose, are sent because a college or university, medical school, or law school is giving preferential treatment to persons who are less qualified now because they are asssumed to have been denied equal basic educational opportunities in the past.

As one would expect, conceptions of human dignity tell us how things like welfare checks or affirmative action acceptance letters should be distributed or whether they should be distributed at all. Obviously, we all have an interest in how things should be distributed or whether they should be distributed at all, since as long as such programs as welfare or affirmative action continue to exist in our society either we or our family or our friends will stand to benefit from them, or we will have to pay for them. In either case, we have an interest in whether such programs can be justified.

Now our three conceptions of human dignity obviously have something to say about the distribution of such things as welfare checks and affirmative action acceptance letters.

A Libertarian Conception of Human Dignity

Consider first a libertarian conception of human dignity. This is the conception that takes liberty as the ultimate political ideal.[25] Here liberty is understood to be the state of being unconstrained by other persons from doing what one wants. Now this definition of liberty limits its scope in two ways. First, not all constraints from whatever source count as a restriction of liberty; the constraints must come from other persons. For example, persons who are constrained by natural forces from getting to the top of Mount Everest are not lacking liberty in this regard. Second, constraints which have their source in other persons but which do not run counter to a particular person's wants, constrain without restricting that person's liberty. Thus, for people who do not want to hear Beethoven's Fifth Symphony, the fact that others have effectively proscribed its performance does not restrict their liberty, even though it does constrain what they are able to do.

Of course, libertarians may want to argue that even such constraints can be seen to restrict a person's liberty once we take into account the general desire or want people normally have to be unconstrained by others. But other philosophers have thought that the possibility of such constraints points to a serious defect in this definition of liberty which only can be remedied by defining liberty more broadly as "the state of being unconstrained by other persons from doing what one is able to do."[26] Applying this latter definition to the above example, we find that people's liberty to hear Beethoven's Fifth Symphony would be restricted, even if they did not want to hear the Symphony (and even if, perchance, they did not want to be unconstrained by others), since other people would still be constraining them from doing what they are able to do.

Confident that problems of defining liberty can be overcome in some satisfactory manner, libertarians go on to characterize their political ideal as requiring that each person is to have the greatest amount of liberty commensurate with the same liberty for all. Given this ideal, libertarians claim that only a limited role for government can be justified. That role, put negatively, is to prevent and punish acts of initial coercion, that is, acts restricting liberty, which are the only wrongful acts for libertarians. Put positively, the role of government is to ensure a right to life, a right to freedom of speech, press, and assembly, and a right to acquire property, typically by voluntary transactions but also through initial acquisition.

It is important to realize, however, that according to the libertarian conception of human dignity, a right to life is not a right to be provided with the means to sustain one's life. Rather, it is simply a right not to be killed unjustly.[27] In fact, there are no welfare rights on the libertarian view, and, hence, no right to receive welfare checks. Thus, libertarians are not in favor of distributing welfare checks except possibly for reasons of charity.

For similar reasons, it is said that there is no right to equal basic educational opportunities under a libertarian conception of human dignity. The basic educational opportunities one has under a libertarian conception of human dignity are usually a function of the property one controls, and since unequal property distributions are said to be justified under a libertarian conception of human dignity, unequal basic educational opportunities are also regarded as justified. But if that is the case, there also cannot be any right to affirmative action, since affirmative action programs are generally designed to correct for failure to provide equal basic educational opportunities in the past. Accordingly, libertarians would not be in favor of distributing affirmative action acceptance letters either, except possibly for reasons of charity.

To better appreciate the libertarian view, let us consider a few examples which defenders of a libertarian conception of human dignity have advanced to justify it. The first two are taken from the economist Milton Friedman, the last from Robert Nozick, a noted libertarian philosopher.[28]

Suppose that you and three friends are walking along the street and you happen to notice and retrieve a $100 bill lying on the pavement. Suppose a rich fellow has been by earlier throwing away $100 bills, and you have been lucky enough to find one of them. Now according to Friedman, it would be nice of you to share your good fortune with your friends, but they have no right that you do so and, hence, they would not be justified in forcing you to share the $100 bill with them. Similarly, Friedman would have us believe that it would be nice of us to provide welfare to the less fortunate members of our society; nevertheless, the less fortunate members have no right to welfare and, hence, they would not be justified in forcing us to provide it.

The second example, which Friedman regards as analogous to the first, involves supposing that there are four Robinson Crusoes, each marooned on four uninhabited islands in the same neighborhood. One of these Robinson Crusoes happens to land on a large and fruitful island which enables him to live easily and well. The others happen to land on tiny and rather barren islands from which they can barely scratch a living. Suppose one day they discover the existence of each other. Now according to Friedman, it would be nice of the fortunate Robinson Crusoe to share the resources of his island with the other three Crusoes, but the other three Crusoes have no right that he share those resources, and it would be wrong for them to force him to do so. Correspondingly, Friedman thinks it would be nice of us to provide the less fortunate in our society with welfare, but the less fortunate have no right that we do so, and it would be wrong for them to force us to do so.

In the third example, Robert Nozick asks us to imagine that we are in a society that has just distributed income according to some ideal pattern, possibly a pattern of equality. We are to further imagine that in such a society Wilt Chamberlain offers to play basketball for us provided that he receives a quarter from every home game ticket that is sold. Suppose we agree to these terms and a million people attend the home games to see Wilt Chamberlain play, thereby giving him an income of $250,000. Since such an income would surely upset the initial pattern of distribution, whatever that happened to be, Nozick contends that this illustrates how an ideal of liberty upsets the patterns required by other conceptions of human dignity and, hence, calls for their rejection.

A Socialist Conception of Human Dignity

So much, then, for a defense of a libertarian conception of human dignity. Let us turn now to our second conception of human dignity, the socialist conception. This is the conception that takes equality as the ultimate political ideal. More precisely, the ideal is equality of need fulfillment. As Karl Marx stated the ideal over a century ago, distribution is to proceed according to the principle from each according to his or her ability, to each according to his or her needs.[29]

Certainly, at first hearing, this conception might sound simply crazy to someone brought up in a capitalist society. For the obvious objection to this conception is that you cannot get persons to contribute according to their ability if you are going to distribute income on the basis of persons' needs rather than on the basis of their contributions. The answer to this objection, according to a socialist conception of human dignity, is to make the work that must be done in a society enjoyable in itself, insofar as this is possible. People will then want to do the work they are capable of doing because they will find it intrinsically rewarding. For a start, socialists might try to get people to accept presently existing, intrinsically rewarding jobs at lower salaries. For example, socialists might try to get top executives to work for $400,000 rather than $800,000 per year. Yet, ultimately, socialists hope to make all jobs as intrinsically rewarding as possible so that, after people are no longer working primarily for external rewards when making their best contributions to society, distribution can proceed on the basis of need.

Socialists propose to implement their conception of human dignity, in part, by giving workers democratic control over the workplace.[30] The key idea here is that if workers have more to say about how they do their work, their work itself will be more intrinsically rewarding. As a consequence, they will be more motivated to work since their work itself will be meeting their needs. Socialists believe that this extension of democracy will lead to a socialization of the means of production and the end of private property, but this need not be the case. It seems perfectly possible to give workers more control over their workplace at the same time that the ownership of the means of production remains in private hands. Of course, private ownership would have a somewhat different character in a society with democratic control of the workplace, but it need not cease to be private ownership. After all, private ownership would also have a somewhat different character in a society with a more equal distribution of private holdings and, hence, a more equal distribution of bargaining power, without ceasing to be private ownership.

Still, even with democratic control of the workplace, there will be some jobs that probably cannot be made intrinsically rewarding, e.g., garbage collecting or changing bedpans. Now what socialists propose to do with respect to such jobs is to divide them up in some equitable manner.[31] Some people might, for example, collect garbage one day each week and then work at intrinsically rewarding jobs the rest of the workweek. Others would change bedpans or do some other slop job one day each week and then work at intrinsically rewarding jobs the other days of the workweek.

So socialists would want to make jobs as intrinsically rewarding as possible, in part through democratic control of the workplace and an equitable assignment of unrewarding tasks. But how would socialists deal with people who not only want an intrinsically rewarding job but also want the rewards that come from a good income. Without providing income differentials, how would socialists motivate such people to contribute according to their ability?

Surely socialists would grant that some income differentials would be necessary to motivate people to make their best contributions. But socialists would strive to keep such differentials to a minimum by making the more talented members of society keenly aware of the social costs of instituting greater income differentials. That is, they would make it very clear that having greater income differentials would be at the cost of failing to satisfy the basic needs of people who are doing all in their power to legitimately satisfy their own needs. The knowledge that this is the case should provide the more talented members of a society with the moral incentive to oppose greater income differentials, or so socialists would argue. And if some people failed to respond to this moral incentive, socialists would contend that they would be justified in requiring (forcing) them to make whatever contribution is necessary so that the basic needs of everyone can be met.

By combining moral and self-interested reasons in this fashion, socialists hope to provide the necessary incentive to get people to make their best contribution to society. In their appeal to moral incentives, however, socialists are no different from welfare liberals or libertarians, since they all recognize enforceable moral constraints on the pursuit of self-interest. Disagreement between them concerns not the legitimacy of such constraints but, rather, what constraints there should be.

So much, then, for a characterization of a socialist conception of human dignity. Clearly it is by making jobs as intrinsically rewarding as possible and by making workers aware of the relevant moral reasons and by enforcing such reasons that socialists hope to get persons to contribute according to their ability even when distribution proceeds according to needs.

Let us now consider how a socialist conception of human dignity relates to the issues of welfare and affirmative action. Would a socialist conception of human dignity support a right to welfare? Obviously it would. Socialists would surely want to distribute welfare checks. But socialists would also want to claim that such a right does not go far enough: it does not provide for persons' nonbasic needs as well as for their basic needs. Likewise, a socialist conception of human dignity would justify a right to affirmative action when persons are less qualified now because they were denied equal basic educational opportunities in the past. Hence, socialists would also want to distribute affirmative action acceptance letters. But, again, socialists would want to claim that such a right does not go far enough, since it does not require a program for restructuring jobs and socializing the means of production.[32]

Finally, it is important to notice that a socialist conception of human dignity does not accord with what exists in countries like Russia or Albania. Judging the acceptability of a socialist conception of human dignity by what takes place in countries like Russia or Albania, where national planning is pursued without worker control, would be just as unfair as judging the acceptability of a libertarian conception of human dignity by what takes place in countries like Chile or South Korea, where citizens are arrested and imprisoned without cause. By analogy, it would be like judging the merits of college football by the way Vanderbilt's team plays or Northwestern's team plays, rather than by the way Penn State's team plays or, at least until recently, the way Notre Dame's team plays. Actually, a fairer comparison would be to judge a socialist conception of human dignity by what takes place in countries like Sweden or Yugoslavia, and to judge a libertarian conception of human dignity by what takes place in the United States. But even these comparisons are not quite appropriate, since none of these countries fully conforms to these conceptions of human dignity.

From Marx to the present, defenders of a socialist conception of human dignity have frequently supported their view by attacking the nonsocialist conceptions of human dignity that most closely resemble it. The favored strategy has been to show that these conceptions of human dignity are inadequate in ways their defenders should have been able to recognize. Utilizing this approach, the political theorist C.B. Macpherson argues that the right to self-development endorsed by both welfare liberals and socialists is only compatible with a socialist conception of human dignity.[33] According to Macpherson, capitalism encourages people to acquire the power to extract benefit from others, and this extractive power is usually acquired at the expense of the self-development of those over whom the power is exercised. Thus, under capitalism the extractive power of some is said to be increased at the expense of the developmental power of others, and while those whose extractive power is increased usually do experience an increase in developmental power as well, Macpherson claims, a net loss of developmental power still obtains overall. Nor is it enough for the defender of a welfare liberal conception of human dignity to show that the transfer of power under capitalism allows for greater self-development than was possible under previous politico-economic systems. For the relevant goal is maximal self-development and only with the elimination of all extractive power under a socialist conception of human dignity, Macpherson claims, can that goal be reached.

More recently, Macpherson has attempted to defend a socialist conception of human dignity by more broadly construing a right to property.[34] Under libertarian and welfare liberal conceptions, a right to property is narrowly construed as a right to exclude others from the use or benefit of particular things. Yet, as the examples of common property and state property indicate, the right to property can be broadened to include as well a right not to be excluded by others from the use or benefit of particular things. From this broader conception of a right to property, Macpherson thinks that a right to self-development, one whose protection requires socialism, can be shown to follow.

A major difficulty with this defense is that Macpherson does not sufficiently consider whether or not the right to self-development on which the socialist conception of human dignity is founded might itself justifiably be limited, as libertarians claim, by a right to liberty. In his discussion of alternative conceptions of liberty, Macpherson does criticize various formulations of negative liberty, but in the main he simply endorses a conception of positive liberty which entails a right to self-development. Macpherson never tries to meet the defenders of negative liberty on their own terms and show that even given a reasonable construal of their own ideal, a right to liberty would naturally lead to a right to self-development.

As one might expect, there have been other attempts to defend a socialist conception of human dignity that appeal more directly to an ideal of liberty. The philosopher Carol C. Gould regards socialist justice as rooted in a conception of positive liberty understood as "the fullest self-realization of social individuals."[35] For, according to Gould, socialist justice "refers to social relations in which no agents deprive any others of the conditions of their positive freedom."[36] Since every individual has a capacity for self-realization simply in virtue of being human, Gould argues, no individual has more of a right to the conditions for the fulfillment of this capacity than any other. Thus, an equal right to positive liberty or freedom is said to be at the heart of socialist justice. Such a right, Gould argues, requires among other things equal access to the means of production and, hence, is incompatible with capitalism.

Unfortunately, Gould does not sufficiently take into account the challenge to a socialist conception of human dignity raised by defenders of negative freedom. She seems content to point out that defenders of negative freedom usually ignore or misrepresent the ideal of positive freedom. Yet she does not give any compelling reason why defenders of negative freedom should recognize the requirements of a socialist conception of human dignity.

A Welfare Liberal Conception of Human Dignity

So much for a defense of a socialist conception of human dignity. Let us turn now to our third conception of human dignity, the welfare liberal conception. As I noted before, the ultimate political ideal for a welfare liberal conception of human dignity is a blend of liberty and equality which can be characterized as fairness or, better, as contractual fairness. More precisely, a welfare liberal conception of human dignity can be understood as maintaining that the fundamental rights and duties in a society are those that people would agree to under fair conditions.[37]

Notice that this conception does not say that the fundamental rights and duties in a society are those to which people actually do agree. For the rights and duties to which people actually do agree might not be fair at all. For example, people might agree to a certain system of fundamental rights and duties only because they have been forced to do so or because their only alternative is starving to death. So actual agreement is not sufficient, nor is it even necessary, for determining a welfare liberal conception of justice; what is necessary and sufficient is that people would agree to such rights and duties under fair conditions.

But what are fair conditions for agreement? According to the philosopher John Rawls, the most prominent contemporary defender of this conception of human dignity, specifying fair conditions for agreement requires an account of (1) a well-ordered society with respect to which agreement is made, (2) the persons making the agreement, and (3) an original position in which the agreement is made.[38]

A Well-Ordered Society

A well-ordered society with respect to which a fair agreement is made is characterized by Rawls in the following manner. First, it is a society that is effectively regulated by a public conception of justice such that everyone accepts, and knows that others likewise accept, the same principles of justice. In addition, the basic institutions of the society satisfy, and are believed by all to satisfy, the same public conception of justice.

Second, it is a society whose members are, and so regard themselves, as free and equal moral persons. They are moral in that, once they have reached the age of reason, each has, and views the others as having, an effective sense of justice. They are equal in that they regard each other as having a right to determine, upon due reflection, the principles of justice by which the basic institutions of their society are to be governed. Lastly, they are free in that they think of themselves both as entitled to make claims on the design of their common institutions in the name of their fundamental aims and interests, and as not inevitably tied to the pursuit of the particular final ends they have at any given time but, rather, as capable of revising and changing those ends on reasonable and rational grounds.

Third, it is a society that is stable with respect to its conception of justice, in that its basic institutions generate an effective sense of justice. In such a society, coercive sanctions are rarely, if ever, actually applied since offenses are infrequent.

Fourth, it is a society that exists under the circumstances of justice. Objectively, this means that conditions of moderate scarcity obtain. Subjectively, this means that persons and groups within the society have a diversity of fundamental interests and ends, and a variety of opposing and incompatible basic beliefs which seem bound to persist in the absence of a sustained and coercive use of power that aims to enforce unanimity.

A Conception of the Person

The persons making a fair agreement are conceived by Rawls as having two powers: the capacity for a sense of justice and the capacity for a conception of the good. The capacity for a sense of justice is the capacity to understand, to apply, and normally to be moved by an effective desire to act from (and not merely in accordance with) the principles of justice as the fair terms of social cooperation. The capacity for a conception of the good is the capacity to form, to revise, and rationally to pursue such a conception, that is, a conception of what we regard as a worthwhile human life. Persons so conceived are also said to have highest-order interests in promoting the full exercise of these two powers and a subordinate interest in advancing their conceptions of the good as best they can, whatever they may be.

The Original Position

The original position from which fair agreements are said to emerge is essentially characterized by a veil of ignorance. This veil deprives persons so situated of the knowledge of their natural and social assets. It also deprives them of the knowledge of their conception of the good and their particular psychological dispositions and propensities. We all know that judges sometimes ask jurors to discount certain information they have heard so that they can reach fair decisions. The veil of ignorance simply generalizes this practice, maintaining that if we are to have fair conditions for determining principles of justice, we too must discount or imagine ourselves to be ignorant of certain information about ourselves when reaching agreement concerning principles of justice.

The veil of ignorance is also assumed to be as thick as possible. This means that persons in the original position are not privy to any information unless that information is absolutely necessary for reaching a rational agreement. In addition, persons in the original position are not required to apply or to be guided by any prior or antecedent principles of right or justice, but only by what they think is in their interest as far as the limits on information allow them to determine this. So characterized, persons in the original position are neither selfish nor moral. Rather, they are simply motivated to choose principles that best serve their interests under the constraints of the original position.

Following from their highest-order interests in advancing their moral powers, persons in the original position are said to have a preference for "primary goods." These are goods that are generally necessary as social conditions and all-purpose means to enable human beings to realize and exercise their moral powers and to pursue their final ends. More specifically, these goods are of five types: (1) basic liberties such as freedom of thought, liberty of conscience, and freedom of association; (2) freedom of movement and free choice of occupation against a background of diverse opportunities; (3) the powers and prerogatives of offices and positions of responsibility; (4) income and wealth; and (5) the social bases of self-respect. In the original position, deliberation proceeds in terms of these primary goods, and certain priorities are established among them.

According to Rawls, the conceptions of the well-ordered society and the person are fundamental and operate as constraints upon his conception of the original position. But actually the relationship is closer than that since the three conceptions are not logically distinct. First, Rawls's conception of the person is already contained in his characterization of persons in the well-ordered society. To be a "free and equal moral person" in a well-ordered society is to possess and effectively exercise the two powers attributed to persons by Rawls's conception of the person. Second, the conceptions of the well-ordered society and the person can be seen to entail, and not merely constrain, Rawls's conception of the original position because Rawls argues that without the veil of ignorance, "the original position would represent the parties not solely as *free and equal moral persons,* but instead as persons also affected by social fortune and natural accidents."[39] It seems best, therefore, to regard Rawls's three conceptions as alternative ways of specifying his account of fair conditions for agreement.

But what would be agreed to under such conditions? Rawls has argued that maximin principles of justice, which maximize benefit to the least advantaged members of a society, would be chosen in the original position.[40] Others, most notably the economist John Harsanyi, have argued that utilitarian principles of justice which maximize average expected utility would be chosen; and still others have argued that compromise principles which strike a compromise between the more advantaged and the less advantaged members of a society would be chosen.[41] Let us consider each of these views in turn.

Maximin Principles

According to Rawls, the original position is a situation in which the maximin rule for choice under uncertainty applies and, as a result, persons in the original position would choose principles that guarantee the highest possible social minimum. Since the maximin rule assumes that the best one can do is maximize the payoff to the least advantaged position, the principles that would be chosen by persons in the original position are considered to be the same as those a rational person would choose for the design of a society in which her enemy would determine her position, which, of course, would be the least advantaged position. This is not to say that persons in the original position believe that their place in society is so determined, because then their reasoning would be based on false premises and that would be unacceptable. Still, the principles persons would select in both situations would be the same, according to Rawls, because both situations are such that the maximin rule for choice under uncertainty applies.

Rawls argues that the original position possesses, to a striking degree, the three features that make a choice situation appropriate for applying the maximin strategy. Those features are:

(1) There is some reason to discount the probabilities that are arrived at in the choice situation.

(2) The person choosing has a conception of the good such that she cares very little, if anything, for what she might gain above the minimum she can in fact be sure of gaining by following the maximin strategy.

(3) Alternative strategies have outcomes that the person choosing can hardly accept.

According to Rawls, the first feature is characteristic of the original position because persons in the original position would not have any objective grounds for assigning probabilities to their turning up in different positions in society, and it would not be reasonable for persons so situated to rely on any probability assignments in the absence of such grounds. In addition, Rawls argues that since persons in the original position would want their choice of principles to seem reasonable to others, particularly their descendants, they would have still another reason for not relying on probability assignments that would be made in the absence of objective grounds.

In discussing the second feature, Rawls begins by arguing that his principles of justice would guarantee a satisfactory minimum. He then goes on to claim that if basic liberties could be shown to have priority in the original position, persons so situated would have no desire to sacrifice basic liberties for greater shares of other primary goods. Hence, they would be content with the minimum provided by the maximin strategy.

To show that the original position possesses the third feature that characterizes situations where the maximin strategy is said to apply, Rawls simply claims that utilitarian principles of justice, under certain conditions, might lead to serious infractions of liberty, which would be unacceptable to persons in the original position.

Utilitarian Principles

Challenging Rawls's derivation of principles of justice in the original position, John Harsanyi and others have argued that persons so situated would favor principles of justice that maximized average expected utility. Harsanyi claims that persons in the original position would first assign an equal probability to their occupying each particular position in society and then select the alternative with the highest average expected utility. To determine utility assignments, persons in the original position are said to compare what it would be like to have particular distributive shares in society while possessing the subjective tastes of persons who have those shares. Harsanyi further assumes that with the knowledge of the appropriate psychological laws and factual information, persons in the original position would arrive at the same comparative utility judgments from which it would then be possible to determine which alternative maximizes their average expected utility.

For example, consider a society with just the three members, X, Y and Z facing two alternatives with the following utility values:

	Alternative A	Alternative C
X	60	30
Y	10	20
Z	10	20
	80	70

Given these alternatives, Harsanyi thinks that persons in the original position would assume that it was equally probable that they would be either X, Y, or Z and, therefore, would select Alternative A as having the higher average expected utility, even though Alternative C provides the higher social minimum. And if the utility values for two alternatives were the following:

	Alternative B	Alternative C
X	50	30
Y	10	20
Z	10	20
	70	70

Harsanyi thinks that persons in the original position would be indifferent between the alternatives, despite the fact that Alternative C again provides the higher social minimum.

According to Harsanyi, any risk aversion that persons in the original position might have in evaluating alternatives would be reflected in a declining marginal utility for money and other social goods. Thus, in our example, we could imagine that a yearly income of $250,000 may be required to provide a utility of 60 while a yearly income of only $10,000 may be needed for a utility of 10. Similarly, an $80,000 yearly income may be required for a utility of 30 but only a $30,000 yearly income for a utility of 20. Harsanyi thinks that persons in the original position would not be risk averse to inequalities of distribution per se, but only insofar as such inequalities resulted in a lower average expected utility in a society.

Compromise Principles

Others, like myself, have disagreed both with Rawls and Harsanyi concerning choice in the original position. Against Rawls, I have argued that persons in the original position would choose principles of justice that guarantee a high social minimum but not the highest possible social minimum.[42] I claim that persons so situated would realize that there may be a significantly large number of individuals in their society, call them the Free-Riders, who are so satisfied with a lower minimum (e.g., one specified in terms of the satisfaction of basic needs) that although these Free-Riders can attain additional social goods in return for making some additional contribution to their society, they choose instead to pursue other needs and interests. While the Free-Riders are refusing to contribute further to society to receive additional social goods, other members of society, call them the Hard-Toilers, may be contributing as much as they can to society in order to receive their highest attainable share of social goods.

I contend that persons in the original position would favor the Hard-Toilers over the Free-Riders for the following reasons. First, the Free-Riders could make up for their smaller shares of social goods resulting from having a lower minimum simply by contributing to their society. On the other hand, if the Hard-Toilers are making their maximal contribution, they would have no way of compensating themselves for receiving the comparatively smaller share of social goods which would result from having the highest minimum in their society. From the point of view of the original position, therefore, it would be rational to specify the minimum so that the Free-Riders who receive less than they might otherwise receive, and are presumably dissatisfied as a result, would be able to compensate themselves for their lesser shares and their presumed dissatisfaction, if they were to choose to do so. Second, persons in this choice situation could not discount the conflict between Free-Riders and Hard-Toilers as unrealistic. For it would be unrealistic to assume that all members of society would always be willing to support themselves by contributing to society, even when they could derive just the same or more benefit by relying on the contributions of others.

Now there are at least two ways that Rawls might respond to my critique. First, Rawls might explain the preferences of the Free-Riders by saying that they place a greater value on leisure than the Hard-Toilers. Yet even if this were the case, it does not seem to justify allowing the Free-Riders to benefit at the expense of the Hard-Toilers. For it would seem that an adequate conception of justice would no more allow Free-Riders to benefit at the expense of Hard-Toilers than it would allow the envious to benefit at the expense of those in society who are legitimately more fortunate. Second, Rawls might argue, as he has in another context, that to favor the Hard-Toilers over the Free-Riders is "to favor the more fortunate twice over."[43] But to be favored in the distribution of natural advantages and not in the distribution of social advantages is hardly to be favored at all. So it is odd to talk about two distributions of advantages—one natural and one social—as though one could benefit a lot from the first, but hardly at all from the second. Rather, the issue seems to be best put as follows: To what degree should Hard-Toilers be allowed to benefit from the use of their natural and social assets? And here my answer is: As much as possible after basic needs have been met.

In support of the compromise view against Harsanyi, I have argued that even if we assume that persons in the original position are making judgments in terms of utilities and that declining marginal utility of social goods has been taken into account, persons so situated would still have grounds for preferring Alternative C to both Alternatives A and B in the preceding example.[44] This is because there are two factors that persons would take into account in reaching decisions in the original position. One factor is the average utility payoff, and this factor would favor Alternative A. The other factor, however, is the distribution of utility payoffs, and this factor would clearly favor Alternative C. Moreover, given this set of alternatives, it is the second factor that would be decisive for persons in the original position who are seeking to compromise the interests of the more advantaged and the less advantaged members of a society.

Of course, as Kenneth Arrow has pointed out, it is still possible to view the preferences of persons in the original position as maximizing average expected utility, provided that the distribution factor is incorporated into the calculation of utilities.[45] Thus, for example, the distribution factor (DF) might be incorporated into the calculation of utilities in the previous examples as follows:

	Alternative A	Alternative B	Alternative C
X	60	50	30
X	10	10	20
Z	10	10	20
DF	− 10	− 10	+ 5
	70	60	75

Since the standard Von Neumann-Morganstern procedure for assigning utilities in situations of uncertainty can incorporate such a distribution factor into the calculation of utilities, we can view the preferences of persons in the original position for Alternative C over Alternatives A and B as one that maximizes average expected utility.[46]

However, interpreting the preferences of persons in the original position in this way does nothing to establish the moral adequacy of utilitarianism as traditionally conceived. For to introduce a distribution factor into the calculation of utilities over and above the individual utility payoffs is to abandon utilitarianism as traditionally conceived in favor of a form of ideal utilitiarianism. In this particular form of ideal utilitarianism, the standard conflict between justice as a distribution factor and utility as average individual utility payoff is transformed into a conflict between two types of utility. Yet the moral adequacy of utilitarianism as traditionally conceived is not established by the possibility of such a transformation because virtually any moral conflict can be represented as a conflict of utilities. Rather, the adequacy of utilitarianism as traditionally conceived depends on showing that when utilities, as represented in the above form of ideal utilitarianism, conflict, the utility of the average individual payoff always has priority over the utility of the distribution factor. Since, as we have seen, persons in the original position would reject such a priority by preferring Alternative C to Alternatives A and B, this clearly raises a serious challenge to the adequacy of utilitarianism as traditionally conceived.[47]

A Basic Needs Minimum

Given these reasons for favoring the compromise view over the maximin and utilitarian views, it seems clear that persons in the original position would choose to specify a social minimum in terms of the satisfaction of a person's basic needs. Now a person's basic needs are those which must be satisfied in order not to seriously endanger the person's health and sanity. Thus, the needs a person has for food, shelter, medical care, protection, companionship, and self-development are at least in part needs of this sort. Naturally, societies vary in their ability to satisfy a person's basic needs, but the needs themselves would not seem to be similarly subject to variation unless there were a corresponding variation in what constitutes health and sanity in different societies. Consequently, even though the criterion of need would not be an acceptable standard for distributing all social goods because, among other things, of the difficulty of determining both what a person's nonbasic needs are and how they should be arranged according to priority, the criterion does appear to be an acceptable standard for determining the minimum of goods and resources each person has a right to receive or acquire.

Actually, specifying a minimum of this sort seems to be the goal of the poverty index used in the United States since 1964.[48] This poverty index is based on the U.S. Department of Agriculture's Economy Food Plan (for an adequate diet) and on evidence showing that low income families spend about one-third of their income on food. The index is then adjusted from time to time to take into account changing prices. However, in order to accord with the goal of satisfying basic needs, the poverty index would have to be further adjusted to take into account (1) that the Economy Food Plan was developed for "temporary or emergency use" and is inadequate for a permanent diet, and (2) that according to recent evidence, low income families spend one-fourth rather than one-third of their income on food.[49]

Of course, one might think that a minimum should be specified in terms of a standard of living that is purely conventional and varies over time and between societies. Benn and Peters, following this approach, have suggested specifying a minimum in terms of the income received by the most numerous group in a society.[50] For example, in the United States today the greatest number of household units falls within the $25,000 to $34,999 bracket (in 1983 dollars).[51] Specifying a minimum in this way, however, leads to certain difficulties. Suppose that the most numerous group of household units in a society with the wealth of the United States fell within a $1,000-$1,499 income bracket (in 1983 dollars). Certainly, it would not thereby follow that a guarantee of $1,500 per household unit would constitute an acceptable minimum for such a society. Or suppose that the income of the most numerous group of household units in such a society fell within the $95,000-$99,999 income bracket (in 1983 dollars). Certainly, a minimum of $100,000 per household unit would not thereby be required. Moreover, there seem to be similar difficulties with any attempt to specify an acceptable minimum in a purely conventional manner.

Nevertheless, it still seems that an acceptable minimum should vary over time and between societies at least to some degree. For example, it could be argued that today a car is almost a necessity in the typical North American household; this was not true fifty years ago, nor is it true today in most other areas of the world. Happily, a basic needs approach to specifying an acceptable minimum can account for such variation without introducing any variation into the definition of the basic needs themselves. Instead, variation enters into the cost of satisfying these needs at different times and in different societies.[52] For in the same society at different times and in different societies at the same time, the normal costs of satisfying a person's basic needs can and do vary considerably. These variations are due in large part to the different ways in which the most readily available means for satisfying people's basic needs are produced. For example, in more affluent societies, the most readily available means for satisfying a person's basic needs are usually processed so as to satisfy nonbasic needs at the same time that they satisfy basic needs. This processing is carried out to make the means more attractive to persons in higher income brackets who can easily afford the extra cost. As a result, the most readily available means for satisfying people's basic needs are much more costly in more affluent societies than they are in less affluent societies. This occurs most obviously with respect to the most readily available means for satisfying people's basic needs for food, shelter, and transportation, but it also occurs with respect to the most readily available means for satisfying people's basic needs for companionship, self-esteem, and self-development. For a person cannot normally satisfy even these latter needs in more affluent societies without participating in at least some relatively costly educational and social development practices. Accordingly, there will be considerable variation in the normal costs of satisfying a person's basic needs as a society becomes more affluent over time, and considerable variation at the same time in societies at different levels of affluence. Consequently, a basic needs approach to specifying an acceptable minimum would guarantee each person the goods and resources necessary to meet the normal costs of satisfying her basic needs in the society in which she lives.

Specifying a social minimum in this way, a welfare liberal conception of human dignity would justify a right to welfare and, hence, would require the distribution of welfare checks to those who, through no fault of their own, need such assistance. It is also clear that this conception of human dignity would justify a right to affirmative action and, hence, require the distribution of affirmative action acceptance letters to those who are less qualified now because they were denied equal basic educational opportunities in the past.

We have now considered all three conceptions of human dignity and related them to the issues of welfare and affirmative action. A libertarian conception which takes liberty to be the ultimate political ideal appears to reject both a right to welfare and a right to affirmative action. A socialist conception which takes equality to be the ultimate political ideal endorses both a right to welfare and a right to affirmative action but appears to regard such rights as only minimal requirements. Only a welfare liberal conception of human dignity which takes a blend of liberty and equality to be the ultimate political ideal appears to endorse both a right to welfare and a right to affirmative action as its principal requirements.

A Practical Reconciliation

Faced with such striking differences, some philosophers, like Alasdair MacIntyre, have argued that these conceptions of human dignity cannot be reasonably reconciled.[53] I contend, however, that a reconciliation is possible, at least at the practical level. Practically speaking, it does not matter whether one endorses liberty, equality, or contractual fairness as the ultimate political ideal because all three of these ideals, when correctly interpreted, support the same practical requirements; and these turn out to be the standardly acknowledged practical requirements of a welfare liberal conception of human dignity, namely, a right to welfare and a right to affirmative action.

Libertarianism

To see that this is the case, let us begin with the ideal of liberty of a libertarian conception of human dignity. As we have seen, libertarians maintain that this ideal justifies neither a right to welfare nor a right to affirmative action. Yet consider a typical conflict situation between the rich and the poor. In this conflict situation, the rich, of course, have more than enough resources to satisfy their basic needs. By contrast, the poor lack the resources to meet their most basic nutritional needs even though they have tried all the legal means available to them for acquiring such resources. Under circumstances like these, libertarians usually maintain that the rich should have the liberty to use their resources to satisfy their luxury needs if they so wish. Libertarians recognize that this liberty might well be enjoyed at the expense of the satisfaction of the most basic nutritional needs of the poor. Libertarians just think that liberty always has priority over other political and social ideals, and since they assume that the liberty of the poor is not at stake in such conflict situations, it is easy for them to conclude that the rich should not be required to sacrifice their liberty so that the basic nutritional needs of the poor may be met.

Of course, libertarians would allow that it would be nice of the rich to share their surplus resources with the poor, just as Friedman would allow that it would be nice of you to share a $100 bill you found with your friends, and nice of the lucky Robinson Crusoe to share his resources with the unlucky Robinson Crusoes. Nevertheless, according to libertarians, such acts of charity are not required because the liberty of the poor is not thought to be at stake in such conflict situations.

In fact, however, the liberty of the poor is at stake. What is at stake is the liberty of the poor to take from the surplus possessions of the rich what is necessary to satisfy their basic nutritional needs. When libertarians are brought to see that this is the case, they are genuinely surprised, one might even say rudely awakened, for they had not previously seen the conflict between the rich and the poor as a conflict of liberties.

Now when the conflict between the rich and the poor is viewed as a conflict of liberties, we can either say that the rich should have the liberty to use their surplus resources for luxury purposes, or we can say that the poor should have the liberty to take from the rich what they require to meet their basic nutritional needs. If we choose one liberty, we must reject the other. What needs to be determined, therefore, is which liberty is morally preferable: the liberty of the rich or the liberty of the poor. I submit that the liberty of the poor, which is the liberty to take from the surplus resources of others what is required to meet one's basic nutritional needs, is morally preferable to the liberty of the rich, which is the liberty to use one's surplus resources for luxury purposes. To see that this is the case we need only appeal to one of the most fundamental principles of morality, one that is common to all political perspectives, namely, the "ought implies can" principle. According to this principle, people are not morally required to do what they lack the power to do or what would involve so great a sacrifice that it would be unreasonable to ask them to perform such an action.[54] For example, suppose I promised to attend a departmental meeting on Friday, but on Thursday I am involved in a serious car accident which puts me into a coma. Surely it is no longer the case that I ought to attend the meeting now that I lack the power to do so. Or suppose instead that on Thursday I develop a severe case of pneumonia for which I am hospitalized. Surely I could claim that I no longer ought to attend the meeting on the grounds that the risk to my health involved in attending is a sacrifice that it would be unreasonable to ask me to bear.

Now, it seems clear that the poor have it within their power to willingly relinquish such an important liberty as the liberty to take from the rich what they require to meet their basic nutritional needs. Nevertheless, it would be unreasonable to ask them to make so great a sacrifice. In the extreme case, it would involve asking the poor to sit back and starve to death. Of course, the poor may have no real alternative to relinquishing this liberty. To do anything else may involve worse consequences for themselves and their loved ones, and may invite a painful death. Accordingly, we may expect that the poor would acquiesce, albeit unwillingly, to a political system that denied them the welfare rights supported by such a liberty, at the same time that we recognize that such a system imposed an unreasonable sacrifice upon the poor—a sacrifice that we could not morally blame the poor for trying to evade.[55] Analogously, we might expect that a woman whose life was threatened would submit to a rapist's demands, at the same time that we recognize the utter unreasonableness of those demands.

By contrast, it would not be unreasonable to ask the rich to sacrifice the liberty to meet some of their luxury needs so that the poor can have the liberty to meet their basic nutritional needs. Of course, we might expect that the rich, for reasons of self-interest and past contribution, might be disinclined to make such a sacrifice. We might even suppose that the past contribution of the rich provides a good reason for not sacrificing their liberty to use their surplus for luxury purposes. Yet, unlike the poor, the rich could not claim that relinquishing such a liberty involved so great a sacrifice that it would be unreasonable to ask them to make it; unlike the poor, the rich could be morally blameworthy for failing to make such a sacrifice. Consequently, if we assume that the requirements of morality cannot violate the "ought implies can" principle, it follows that, despite what libertarians claim, the right to liberty endorsed by libertarians actually favors the liberty of the poor over the liberty of the rich.

Yet libertarians might object to this conclusion, claiming that it would be unreasonable to ask the rich to sacrifice the liberty to meet some of their luxury needs so that the poor could have the liberty to meet their basic nutritional needs. As I have pointed out, libertarians do not usually see the situation as a conflict of liberties, but suppose they did. How plausible would such an objection be? Not very plausible at all, I think. For consider: what are libertarians going to say about the poor? Is it not clearly unreasonable to ask the poor to sacrifice the liberty to meet their basic needs so that the rich can have the liberty to meet their luxury needs? Is it not clearly unreasonable to ask the poor to sit back and starve to death? If it is, then there is no resolution of this conflict that it would be reasonable to ask both the rich and the poor to accept. But that would mean that the libertarian ideal of liberty cannot be a moral ideal; for a moral ideal resolves conflicts of interest in ways that it would be reasonable to ask everyone affected to accept. As long as libertarians think of themselves as putting forth a moral ideal, therefore, they cannot allow that it would be unreasonable *both* to ask the rich to sacrifice the liberty to meet some of their luxury needs in order to benefit the poor and to ask the poor to sacrifice the liberty to meet their basic needs in order to benefit the rich. But I submit that if one of these requests is to be judged reasonable, then, by any neutral assessment, it must be the request that the rich sacrifice the liberty to meet some of their luxury needs so that the poor can have the liberty to meet their basic needs; there is no other plausible resolution, if libertarians intend to be putting forth a moral ideal.

It should also be noted that this case for restricting the liberty of the rich depends upon the willingness of the poor to take advantage of whatever opportunities are available to them for satisfying their basic needs by engaging in mutually beneficial work, so that failure of the poor to take advantage of such opportunities would normally either cancel or at least significantly reduce the obligation of the rich to restrict their own liberty for the benefit of the poor.[56] In addition, the poor would be required to return the equivalent of any surplus possessions they have taken from the rich once they are able to do so and still satisfy their basic needs. Nor would the poor be required to keep the liberty to which they are entitled. They could give up part of it, or all of it, or risk losing it on the chance of gaining a greater share of liberties or other social goods.[57] Consequently, the case for restricting the liberty of the rich for the benefit of the poor is not unconditional, and the rights of the poor in this respect are not inalienable.

Of course, there will be cases where the poor fail to satisfy their basic needs not because of any direct restriction of liberty on the part of the rich, but because the poor are in such dire need that they are unable even to attempt to take from the rich what they require. Accordingly, in such cases, the rich would not be performing any act of commission that prevents the poor from taking what they require. Yet even in such cases, the rich would normally be performing acts of commission that prevent other persons from aiding the poor by taking from the surplus possessions of the rich. And when assessed from a moral point of view, restricting the liberty of these other persons would not be morally justified for the very same reason that restricting the liberty of the poor to meet their own basic needs would not be morally justified: it would not be reasonable to ask all of those affected to accept such a restriction of liberty.

Nevertheless, libertarians might respond that even supposing that a right to welfare could be morally justified on the basis of the liberty of the poor to take from the rich in order to meet their basic needs and the liberty of third parties to take from the rich in order to provide for the basic needs of the poor, the poor still would be better off without the enforcement of such a right.[58] For example, it might be argued that when people are not forced through taxation to support a right to welfare, they are both more productive, since they are able to keep more of what they produce, and more charitable, since they tend to give more freely to those in need when they are not forced to do so. As a result, so the argument goes, the poor would benefit more from the increased charity of a libertarian society than they would from the guaranteed minimum of a welfare state.

Yet, surely it is difficult to comprehend how the poor could be better off in a libertarian society, assuming, as seems likely, that they would experience a considerable loss of self-respect once they had ultimately to depend upon the uncertainties of charity rather than a guaranteed minimum for the satisfaction of their basic needs. It is also difficult to comprehend how people who are so opposed to a guaranteed minimum would turn out to be so charitable to the poor in a libertarian society.

Moreover, in a libertarian society, the provision of welfare would involve an impossible coordination problem. For if the duty to provide welfare to the poor is at best supererogatory, as libertarians claim, then no one can legitimately force anyone who does not consent to provide such welfare. The will of the majority on this issue could not be legitimately imposed upon dissenters.[59] Assuming, then, that the provision of welfare requires coordinated action on a broad front, such coordination could not be achieved in a libertarian society because it would require a near unanimous agreement of all its members.[60]

Nevertheless, it might still be argued that the greater productivity of the more talented people in a libertarian society would provide increased employment opportunities and increased voluntary welfare assistance that would benefit the poor more than a guaranteed minimum would in a welfare state. But this simply could not occur. For if the more talented members of a society provided sufficient employment opportunities and voluntary welfare assistance to enable the poor to meet their basic needs, then the conditions for invoking a right to a guaranteed minimum in a welfare state would not arise, since the poor are first required to take advantage of whatever employment opportunities and voluntary welfare assistance are available to them before they can legitimately invoke such a right. Consequently, when sufficient employment opportunities and voluntary welfare assistance obtain, there would be no practical difference in this regard between a libertarian society and a welfare state, since neither would justify invoking a right to a guaranteed minimum. Only when insufficient employment opportunities and voluntary welfare assistance obtain, would there be a practical difference between a libertarian society and a welfare state, and then it would clearly benefit the poor to be able to invoke the right to a guaranteed minimum. Consequently, given the conditional nature of the right to a guaranteed minimum and the practical possibility (in most cases, the actuality) of insufficient employment opportunities and voluntary welfare assistance obtaining, there is no reason to think that the poor would be better off without the enforcement of a right to welfare.[61]

In brief, what this shows is that if liberty is taken to be the ultimate political ideal, then, contrary to what libertarians claim, a right to welfare would not only be morally required, but would clearly benefit the poor as well.

The same would hold true if libertarians were to define liberty in terms of rights. For the most important ultimate rights in terms of which liberty would be specified are, according to this view, a right to life understood as a right not to be killed unjustly and a right to property understood as a right to acquire goods and resources either by initial acquisitions or voluntary transactions. Now in order to evaluate this view, we must determine what are the practical implications of these rights.

Presumably, a right to life understood as a right not to be killed unjustly would not be violated by defensive measures designed to protect one's person from life-threatening attacks. Yet would this right be violated when the rich prevent the poor from taking what they require to satisfy their basic nutritional needs? Obviously, as a consequence of such preventive actions poor people sometimes do starve to death. Have the rich, then, in contributing to this result, killed the poor, or simply let them die; and, if they have killed the poor, have they done so unjustly?

Now sometimes the rich, in preventing the poor from taking what they require to meet their basic nutritional needs, would not in fact be killing the poor, but only causing them to be physically or mentally debilitated. Yet, since such preventive acts involve resisting the life-preserving activities of the poor, when the poor do die as a consequence of such acts, it seems clear the the rich would be killing the poor, whether intentionally or unintentionally.

Of course, libertarians would want to argue that such killing is simply a consequence of the legitimate exercise of property rights, and hence not unjust. But to understand why libertarians are mistaken in this regard, let us appeal again to that fundamental principle of morality, the "ought implies can" principle. In this context, the principle can be used to assess two opposing accounts of property rights. According to the first account, a right to property is *not* conditional upon whether other persons have sufficient opportunities and resources to satisfy their basic needs. This view holds that the initial acquisition and voluntary transactions of some can leave others, through no fault of their own, dependent upon charity for the satisfaction of their most basic needs. By contrast, according to the second account, initial acquisition and voluntary transactions can confer title to all goods and resources except those surplus goods and resources of the rich that are required to satisfy the basic needs of those poor who, through no fault of their own, lack the opportunities and resources to satisfy their own basic needs.

Clearly, only the first of these two accounts of property rights would generally justify the killing of the poor as a legitimate exercise of the property rights of the rich. Yet it would be unreasonable to ask the poor to accept anything other than some version of the second account of property rights. Moreover, according to the second account, it does not matter whether the poor would actually die or are only physically or mentally debilitated as a result of such acts of prevention. Either result would preclude property rights from arising. Of course, the poor may have no real alternative to acquiescing in a political system modeled after the first account of property rights, even though such a system imposes an unreasonable sacrifice upon them—a sacrifice that we could not blame them for trying to evade. At the same time, although the rich would be disinclined to do so, it would not be unreasonable to ask them to accept a political system modeled after the second account of property rights—the account favored by the poor. Consequently, if we assume that the requirements of morality cannot violate the "ought implies can" principle, it follows that, despite what libertarians claim, the right to life and the right to property endorsed by libertarians actually support a right to welfare.

Nevertheless, it might be objected that the right to welfare that has been established against the libertarian is not the same as the right to welfare endorsed by the welfare liberal. We could mark this difference by referring to the welfare right that has been established against the libertarian as "a negative welfare right" and referring to the welfare right endorsed by the welfare liberal as "a positive welfare right." The significance of this difference is that a person's negative welfare right can be violated only when other people through acts of commission interfere with a person's exercise of that right, whereas a person's positive welfare right can be violated by such acts of commission, but also by acts of omission. However, this difference will have little practical import. For once libertarians come to recognize the legitimacy of a negative welfare right, then in order not to be subject to the poor person's discretion in choosing when and how to exercise her negative welfare right, libertarians will tend to favor two morally legitimate ways of preventing the exercise of such rights. First, libertarians can provide the poor with mutually beneficial job opportunities. Second, libertarians can institute an adequate positive welfare right that would take precedence over the poor person's negative welfare right. Accordingly, if libertarians adopt either or both of these ways of legitimately preventing the poor from exercising their negative welfare rights, libertarians will end up endorsing the same sort of welfare institutions favored by welfare liberals. By a similar argument, it can be shown that an ideal of liberty also supports a requirement of equal basic educational opportunities and, when such opportunities have been denied in the past, a requirement of affirmative action.

Now it is possible that libertarians convinced to some extent by the foregoing arguments might want to accept a right to welfare and a right to the basic educational opportunities that are necessary for the satisfaction of one's basic needs, but then deny that there is a right to *equal* basic educational opportunities. Such a stance, however, is only plausible if we restrict the class of morally legitimate claimants to those within a given (affluent) society, for only then would a right to equal basic educational opportunities be different from the right to the basic educational opportunities necessary for the satisfaction of people's basic needs. But once it is recognized that the class of morally legitimate claimants includes, for example, distant peoples and future generations, then even libertarians should grant that guaranteeing the basic educational opportunities necessary for the satisfaction of their basic needs to all morally legitimate claimants would lead to providing them all with roughly equal basic educational opportunities.[62]

Yet even if libertarians were to accept a right to equal basic educational opportunities, they still might want to reject a right to affirmative action for the following reasons. First, libertarians might claim that although serious deprivation of equal basic educational opportunities has occurred in the past, it is enough that we do not deny people such opportunities anymore. We need not provide affirmative action as well. Second, libertarians might claim that although it was wrong to deprive people of equal basic educational opportunities in the past, affirmative action is also wrong in that it deprives white males of legitimate opportunities, and two wrongs do not make a right.

The problem with the first reason is that it is an inconsistent stance to take, since it affirms a right to equal opportunity but then, by ruling out a right to affirmative action, denies the redress that is appropriate when one's right to equal opportunity has been denied. The problem with the second reason is that it fails to take into account the fact that no matter what we do, some rights violations will occur. Thus, although affirmative action does violate the rights of white males to some degree, failing to correct for deprivations of equal basic educational opportunities in the past would involve more serious rights violations. Accordingly, libertarians should be able to realize that affirmative action is simply the lesser of two evils.

What I have shown, therefore, is that a libertarian conception of human dignity supports the same practical requirements as a welfare liberal conception of human dignity. Both favor a right to welfare and a right to affirmative action when persons are less qualified now because they were denied equal basic educational opportunities in the past.

Socialism

Let us now turn to the socialist conception of human dignity. The socialist conception, you will recall, did endorse a right to welfare and a right to affirmative action, but it appeared to endorse these rights only as minimal requirements. In addition, socialists maintain that we are also required to meet nonbasic needs and to socialize the means of production. Nevertheless, I contend that once we see how demanding the requirements of a

welfare liberal conception of human dignity are, (1) the additional requirement to meet nonbasic needs will be seen to have little application, and (2)
the additional requirement to socialize the means of production will be
seen to be completely unnecessary.

In support of the first contention, notice that a welfare liberal conception
of human dignity does not require only that a welfare minimum be
provided in our own society, but also that we take what steps we can to
provide both a welfare minimum to the needy in other societies and the
resources that will be required so that future generations will be able to
meet their basic needs.[63] At present, there is probably a sufficient world-
wide supply of goods and resources to meet the normal costs of satisfying
the basic nutritional needs of all existing persons in the societies in which
they live. According to the former U.S. Secretary of Agriculture, Bob
Bergland: "For the past 20 years, if the available world food supply had
been evenly divided and distributed, each person would have received
more than the minimum of calories."[64] Other authorities have made similar assessments of the available world food supply.[65] In fact, it has been
projected that if all arable land were optimally utilized, a population of
between 38 and 48 billion people could be supported.[66]

Needless to say, the adoption of a policy of meeting the basic nutritional
needs of all existing persons would necessitate significant changes, especially in developed societies. For example, the large percentage of the
U.S. population whose food consumption clearly exceeds even an adequately adjusted poverty index would have to substantially alter their eat-
ing habits. In particular, they would have to reduce their consumption of
beef and pork so as to make more grain available for direct human consumption. (Presently, the amount of grain fed American livestock is as
much as all the people of China and India eat in a year.) Thus, the satisfaction of at least some of the nonbasic needs of the more advantaged in
developed societies would have to be foregone so that the basic nutritional
needs of all existing persons in developing and underdeveloped societies
could be met.

Such changes, however, may still have little effect on the relative costs of
satisfying people's basic needs in different societies. For even after the basic
nutritional needs of all existing persons have been met, the normal costs of
satisfying basic needs would still tend to be greater in developed societies
than in developing and underdeveloped societies. This is because the most
readily available means for satisfying basic needs in developed societies
would still tend to be more processed to satisfy nonbasic needs along with
basic needs. Nevertheless, once the basic nutritional needs of future generations are also taken into account, then the satisfaction of the nonbasic

needs of the more advantaged in developed societies would have to be further restricted in order to preserve the fertility of cropland and other food-related natural resources for the use of future generations.[67] And once basic needs other than nutritional needs are taken into account as well, still further restrictions would be required. For example, it has been estimated that presently a North American uses fifty times more resources than an Indian. This means that in terms of resource consumption, the North American continent's population is the equivalent of 12.5 billion Indians.[68] Obviously, this would have to be radically altered if the basic needs of distant peoples and future generations are to be met. Thus, eventually the practice of utilizing more and more efficient means of satisfying people's basic needs in developed societies would appear to have the effect of *equalizing* the normal costs of meeting people's basic needs across societies.[69]

It can also be shown that if one endorses, as welfare liberals do (1) the welfare rights of distant peoples and future generations, and also accepts (2) an obligation not to bring into existence persons who would lack a reasonable opportunity to lead a good life, then in consistency one should accept (3) an obligation to bring into existence persons who would have a reasonable opportunity to lead a good life. And clearly (3) serves to limit the legitimate use of abortion.

It can be shown that (3) follows from the acceptance of (1) and (2) because any reason we can give for accepting (2) that is consistent with (1) will suggest an analogous reason for supporting (3). This view has been called the "symmetry view," since it maintains that there is a symmetry between an obligation not to procreate and an obligation to procreate, or, as I like to put it, a symmetry between a right not to be born and right to be born.

The grounds for accepting (2), expressed in terms of a right not to be born, have been given by the philosopher Joel Feinberg as follows:

> ...if, before the child has been born, we know that the conditions for the fulfillment of his most basic interests have already been destroyed, and we permit him nevertheless to be born, we become a party to the violations of his rights.
>
> In such circumstances, therefore, a proxy for the fetus might plausibly claim on its behalf, a right not to be born. That right is based on his future rather than his present interests (he has no actual present interests); but of course it is not contingent on his birth because he has it before birth, from the very moment that satisfaction of his most basic future interests is rendered impossible.[70]

Other welfare liberals, like the philosophers Jan Narveson and Derek Parfit, similarly endorse (2). According to Narveson:

> ...I therefore see no reason to deny that a concern for people's rights can dictate a restrictive population policy even though they are the very people who would not have existed had it been in effect.[71]

But could a welfare liberal consistently reject (2)? Such a rejection would involve endorsing the view that coming into existence is neither good nor bad for a person. According to this view, only what happens after one becomes a person can be either good or bad for a person. Thus, for example, being born healthy is neither good nor bad for a person. Moreover, on this view, one does not become a person until sometime after birth, possibly as long as two years after birth. Up until that time, whether a newborn is happy or miserable is not in itself morally relevant. Until it becomes a person, the happiness or misery of a newborn is only morally relevant in virtue of the effects it has on those who are already persons. Consequently, if existing persons would derive a net benefit from the continued existence of a miserable newborn, possibly as an experimental subject, and would, therefore, want to keep the newborn alive until it became a person and thereby acquired a right that its miserable existence be terminated, there would be no moral objection to their doing so. But it is just this eventuality that welfare liberals sought to preclude by affirming (2), and there seems to be no alternative way of guaranteeing this desired result.

Accordingly, challenges to the symmetry view have usually taken a different tack, and have tried to show that it is possible to consistently accept (1) and (2) while rejecting (3); that is, these challenges have attempted to defend what had been called the "asymmetry view." For example, Jan Narveson defends the asymmetry view on the ground that there is a failure of reference in the case of the person who would have a reasonable opportunity to lead a good life.[72] Narveson argues in the following manner:

> If I bring into existence a person who would lack a reasonable opportunity to lead a good life, there will be a person who can reproach me that I did not prevent her leading an unfortunate existence. But if I do not bring into existence a person who would have a reasonable opportunity to lead a good life, there will be no person who can reproach me for preventing her leading a fortunate existence.

Given this failure of reference in the case of the person who would have a reasonable opportunity to lead a good life, Narveson concludes, it would only be wrong to bring into existence a person who would lack a reasonable opportunity to lead a good life.

Unfortunately for Narveson's defense, it is possible to argue analogously:

> If I do not bring into existence a person who would lack a reasonable opportunity to lead a good life, there will be no person who can thank me

> for preventing her from leading an unfortunate existence. And if I do
> bring into existence a person who would have a reasonable opportunity to
> lead a good life, there will be a person who can thank me for not prevent-
> ing her from leading a fortunate existence.

Thus, whatever failure of reference there is, it occurs in both cases and,
hence, it cannot provide a suitable defense for the asymmetry view.

A second attempt to defend the asymmetry view, also advanced by Narveson, begins with the assumption that a person's life cannot be compared
with her nonexistence unless the person already exists. This means that if
one allows a fetus to develop into a person who has a reasonable opportunity to lead a good life, one does not make that person better off than if
she never existed. And it also means that if one allows a fetus to develop
into a person who lacks a reasonable opportunity to lead a good life, one
does not make that person worse off than if she never existed. But what,
then, justifies a right not to be born in the latter case? According to the
argument, it is simply the fact that unless the fetus is aborted, a person will
come into existence who lacks a reasonable opportunity to lead a good life.
But if this fact justifies a right not to be born, why, in the former case,
would the fact that unless the fetus is aborted a person will come into
existence who has a reasonable opportunity to lead a good life not suffice
to justify a right to be born? Clearly, no reason has been given to distinguish the cases.

Furthermore, consider the grounds for aborting a fetus that would develop into a person who lacks a reasonable opportunity to lead a good life.
It is not simply that the person is sure to experience some unhappiness in
her life because in every person's life there is some unhappiness. Rather, it
is that the amount of expected unhappiness in this person's life would
render her life not worth living. This implies that the justification for
aborting in this case is based on a comparison of the value of the person's
life with the value of her nonexistence. For how else can we say that the fact
that the fetus would develop into a person who lacks a reasonable opportunity to lead a good life justifies our preventing the person's very existence? Consequently, this argument depends upon a denial of the very
assumption with which it began, namely, that the person's life cannot be
compared with her nonexistence unless that person already exists.

A third attempt to defend the asymmetry view, proposed by Trudy
Govier, maintains that there is a difference in strength between one's duty
to prevent a fetus from developing into a person who lacks a reasonable
opportunity to lead a good life and one's duty not to prevent a fetus from
developing into a person who has a reasonable opportunity to lead a good
life.[73] For example, it might be argued that the former duty is a relatively

strong duty to prevent harm, whereas the latter duty is a relatively weak duty to promote well-being, and that only the relatively strong duty justifies a correlative right—in this case, a right not to be born. But, even granting that our duty to prevent harm is stronger than our duty to promote well-being, in the case at issue we are dealing not just with a duty to promote well-being, but with a duty to promote *basic* well-being. And, as welfare liberals would be the first to admit, our duty to prevent basic harm and our duty to promote basic well-being are not that distinct from a moral point of view. From which it follows that, if our duty to prevent basic harm justifies a right not to be born in the one case, then our duty to promote basic well-being would justify a right to be born in the other.

Consequently, all three of the attempts we have considered to defend the asymmetry view over the symmetry view fail for reasons which I think will undermine any similar attempt. For whatever reason is given for defending (2) that is consistent with (1) it will always suggest an analogous reason for supporting (3). And (3) severely limits the legitimate use of abortion.[74]

I submit, therefore, that once we distribute resources in accordance with a welfare liberal conception of human dignity so as to meet the basic needs of distant peoples and future generations, and to bring into existence persons who would have a reasonable opportunity to lead a good life, there will be very little left over for the satisfaction of nonbasic needs that a socialist conception of human dignity requires. Of course, the scope of the requirements of a welfare liberal conception of human dignity has not always been appreciated; yet once it is taken into account, the further requirement of a socialist conception of human dignity to meet nonbasic needs as well will be seen to have little application.

With regard to the second contention, as we have seen, it may be necessary to make work more intrinsically rewarding and to introduce moral incentives in order to meet basic needs; but it is not necessary to socialize the means of production. For it would suffice for meeting basic needs simply to distribute more widely the control of goods and resources. Presently, for example, in the United States 57 percent of the total net wealth and 86 percent of total financial assets are owned by 10 percent of all families.[75] Accordingly, to meet basic needs in the United States, it would surely be necessary to change that distribution. Also, to meet the basic needs of people world-wide, it would be necessary to adopt more efficient means for meeting the basic needs of people in affluent societies generally. Surely there are more efficient ways of meeting basic nutritional needs than using so much grain to feed livestock at such a tremendous loss of usable protein. But since all of these requirements for meeting basic needs already follow from a welfare liberal conception of human dignity, I conclude that there is no need to adopt the socialist conception's additional requirement to socialize the means of production. For this additional requirement is completely unnecessary given the demands of a welfare liberal conception of human dignity.

As Marx pointed out, the widespread exploitation of laborers associated with early capitalism only began when large numbers "had been robbed of all their own means of production and of all the guarantees of existence afforded by the old feudal system" by persons and economic groups who already had considerable wealth and power.[76] But the concentration of wealth and power necessary to carry out such exploitation is not likely to be found in a society which, in accordance with a welfare liberal conception of human dignity, provides for the basic needs of all its members as well as for the basic needs of distant peoples, future generations, and those persons who, if they were brought into existence, would have a reasonable opportunity to lead a good life. Consequently, a shift from such restricted private ownership of the means of production to socialization of those means may in fact have little practical consequence.

Approaching the issue in yet another way, it seems clear that for Marx, socializing the means of production is best construed as a means to an end. The end for Marx would be to form "an association in which the free development of each is the condition of the free development of all."[77] But then the question arises as to why we should think that this end is best pursued by socializing the means of production, rather than by widely dispersing the ownership of those means. It might be argued that to bring about such an association would require that individuals be given control over their working conditions (or have the option of controlling those conditions), and that sooner or later this would lead to socializing the means of production. For example, Barry Clark and Herbert Gintis contend that "strengthening the system of total liberties" requires such worker control and would lead to the abolition of capitalism.[78] Yet even supposing that an appropriate degree of worker control were required to form an association in which the free development of each is the condition of the free development of all,[79] why would not such worker control be compatible with a system in which the ownership of the means of production were widely dispersed throughout the society? Under such a system, individuals as investors would each decide how to invest the fairly small shares of capital they owned. Thus, some would want to invest in firms in which they worked so that their own productivity would contribute to a return on their investment. Others would choose not to do so, realizing that they could get a higher return from their investment if they invested their shares of capital elsewhere. Over such investment decisions, however, individuals *as workers* would have no control.[80] But once these decisions had been made, then the rights of individuals as workers would have to be taken into account in designing the business enterprise. For example, a group of in- vestors may decide to form a firm, call it Proletarians United, to produce super-widgets, believing that many people would love to have one. But given such a decision, the workers Proletarians United employs would have to be guaranteed significant control over such features of their working conditions as job descriptions, working hours, and hiring, firing, and pro- motion policies. Nor would it be possible under the proposed system for Proletarians United to extract an unfair advantage from the workers it employs by threatening to replace them with other workers. The reason for this is that as long as the demands for worker control are reasonable and allow for a good return on the investment, workers under the proposed system normally would be able either to find other firms willing to employ them or to pool their own investment holdings and go into business for themselves. Thus, even if an adequate conception of human dignity did require a significant degree of worker control, this requirement would still seem to be perfectly compatible with a system in which the ownership of the means of production were widely dispersed throughout the society.

IV. Conclusion

We can conclude, therefore, that all three conceptions of human dignity that we have considered support the same practical requirements of a right to welfare and a right to affirmative action which are at the heart of the *Economic Pastoral's* policy recommendations. Of course, many people who accept these conceptions of human dignity are not committed to these practical requirements, but that is because they really do not understand that these are the practical requirements of the conceptions of justice they endorse. My hope is that once they are brought to see what their con- ceptions actually do require, they will then take steps to bring their be- havior into accord with their political ideals. For persons failing to take such steps will have to view themselves as unjust and immoral persons, and I am hoping that that is a price most persons will not be willing to pay.

Assuming that people want to be just and moral, as I think they do, showing them that libertarian, welfare liberal, and socialist conceptions of human dignity have the same basic practical requirements as the *Economic Pastoral* is the best approach I know to philosophically defending the bishops' letter. Of course, the bishops reject the view that "an unfettered free-market economy, whose owners, workers, and consumers pursue their enlightened self-interest, provides the greatest possible liberty, material welfare, and equity" that is associated with the libertarian conception of human dignity, as well as the view that "capitalism is inherently inequitable...and must be replaced by a radically different system" that abolishes private property, the profit motive and the free market that is associated with the socialist conception of human dignity.[81] The problem is that they fail to provide any philosophical reasons to justify their rejection of these views. Consequently, by showing that neither of these views requires the type of economic system that is commonly associated with it, the foregoing argument seems to provide just the kind of philosophical justification for the *Economic Pastoral* that the bishops need.

PART 2

Economic Rights Versus Human Dignity: The Flawed Moral Vision of the United States Catholic Bishops

Douglas Rasmussen

The economic challenge of today has many parallels with the political challenge that confronted the founders of our nation. In order to create a new form of political democracy they were compelled to develop ways of thinking and political institutions that had never existed before. Their efforts were arduous and their goals imperfectly realized, but they launched an experiment in the protection of civil and political rights that has prospered through the efforts of those who came after them. *We believe the time has come for a similar experiment in securing economic rights: the creation of an order that guarantees the minimum conditions of human dignity in the economic sphere for every person.*[1]

With these words, the United States Catholic Bishops (hereafter referred to as the "Catholic Bishops") call for nothing less than a moral and social revolution—a revolution that seeks to change not merely how individuals will conduct themselves privately, but the conduct of public policy as well. As the Catholic Bishops state: "The securing of these rights will make demands on *all* members of society, on all private-sector institutions and on government."[2] These economic rights are, in effect, to be granted a status in the cultural and legal tradition of this nation analogous to those rights enumerated in the Bill of Rights.[3] In other words, the Catholic Bishops seek to make these economic rights not merely duties that one person owes another person, but entitlements which are legally enforceable: "Government may levy the taxes necessary to meet these responsibilities, and citizens have a moral obligation to pay those taxes."[4] The rights to life, food, clothing, shelter, rest, medical care, education, employment, healthful working conditions, and fair wages are entitlements that all human beings have and which government has the obligation to enforce. These rights are "empowerments that call for positive action by individuals and society at large."[5] The Catholic Bishops seek, then, to have us engage in what they call "a new American Experiment," and if it is successful, this experiment will profoundly change the principles by which this nation has traditionally determined the function of government.

It goes without saying that the Catholic Bishops have every right to enter into the ongoing debate on public policy. They may, and indeed should, seek to have their views on what government ought to do evaluated and discussed just as one would evaluate and discuss the views of anyone else; for it is not the case that the views of the Catholic Bishops are meant only for those who share their religious vision. "We seek the cooperation and support of those who do not share our faith or tradition."[6] It has always been a Catholic conviction that human understanding and religious belief are complementary and not contradictory, and so Catholic social teaching seeks to support its perspectives on public policy with philosophical argumentation and empirical analysis. The Catholic Bishops' views, therefore, can be evaluated and discussed in terms of the philosophical arguments used and the empirical analyses presented.[7]

The Catholic Bishops' philosophical arguments on behalf of the aforementioned economic rights and their understanding of the American economic system are evaluated in this essay. While supportive of the need for a moral vision from which to critique the American economy and formulate public policy, this essay's basic thesis is that the Catholic Bishops have failed to grasp both the fundamental character of human dignity and the nature of the free market and, as a result, offer a moral vision and an account of the free market that are seriously flawed. The claim by the Catholic Bishops that human beings have economic rights is unjustified, and the new order they would create to secure these alleged rights would itself be an affront to the human dignity with which they are concerned. Simply put, the Catholic Bishops not only do not understand the nature of the free market, they also do not understand the basic character of human morality.

It might seem surprising to those not familiar with moral philosophy and political economy that such a charge should even be made. Yet, the truths of moral philosophy and political economy are not easily attainable, and no one, neither the Catholic Bishops, nor this author, nor anyone else, has omniscience on these matters. This is not to say that knowledge regarding these matters is impossible. Rather, it is only to say that we must work very hard for it, and we should not be surprised that what at first appears simple ends up being extremely complex. The fact that the Catholic Bishops should be accused of failing to understand either the free market or human morality is nothing more, then, than part of the process by which we try to determine the truth regarding these complicated matters, and it is after all how the truth of things stands that concerns us. It is, at least, the concern of this essay.

Though this essay is primarily a critique of the Catholic Bishops' views, there is nonetheless present throughout a sketch of what I take to be the appropriate view of human dignity, and an explanation of why the free market is so well-suited to meeting the conditions human dignity requires. By the end of this essay, the reader should have a fairly clear picture of what alternative moral vision[8] is being advanced and why it is preferable to the one presented by the Catholic Bishops.

I. The Need for a Moral Vision

The Catholic Bishops claim that we need to morally evaluate the American economic system. High interest rates, the federal budget deficit, the international trade deficit, the problems facing American agriculture, the disproportionate rate of unemployment among Black and Hispanic young people, the misuse of natural resources, the 33 million Americans who are poor, and the additional 20 million who are needy are problems that demand moral analysis. "The precarious economic situation of so many people and so many families in this rich nation is cause for examination of our nation's economic arrangements."[9] Just as the Catholic Bishops' 1983 pastoral letter, *The Challenge of Peace: God's Promise and Our Response*, proclaimed the need for defense policies to be evaluated from a moral point of view, the *Economic Pastoral* proclaims a similar need for the American economic system. The economic challenges that we face today and the proposals for meeting them require a moral vision.

Trying to examine the American economic system apart from a moral vision ignores the fact that there are other ways by which economic life can be conducted, and the fact that by subjecting the American economic system to moral scrutiny, the impetus for changes in the economic system is created. This may, of course, be why some might take issue with the Catholic Bishops' *Economic Pastoral*; for to subject anything to moral examination is to be open to the possibility of change. But to refuse to evaluate the American economic system in moral terms is to assume that there is no room for moral improvement in our economic institutions. Regardless of the moral vision one takes, it is hardly plausible to claim that the status quo needs no moral improvement.

Whether it is Socrates questioning the citizens of Athens or Jefferson writing in the Declaration of Independence, moral visions, no matter how minimal, have always carried with them the possibility of change. The status quo is never safe once a moral vision is introduced and, unless we despair of having moral knowledge at all,[10] we need to invoke[11] a moral vision in order to be open to the possibility of improving our lives. Leaving aside for the time being the question of just how one morally evaluates an "economic system," certainly the Catholic Bishops' claim that we need a moral vision from which to evaluate the status quo is something that can be accepted. There is, of course, the danger that by engaging in moral evaluation one can be mistaken and thus propose policies that will make things worse rather than better. We must, therefore, proceed very cautiously when we develop a moral vision. But we must nonetheless proceed.

Before discussing the Catholic Bishops' moral vision in greater detail, it should at least be noted that a moral vision is needed not only in order to evaluate social, political, and economic institutions, but also in order for persons to know the best way to live their lives. Human beings have (to varying degrees) the capacity for full human development and need something that will provide them guidance as they seek to fulfill their potential. It is the task of a moral vision to provide this knowledge, and it is the central task of every person to discover what this moral vision involves for his or her life. A moral vision would be appropriate for human beings even if human life did not involve life among others. Individual human beings need to know what human flourishing is. They need to know in what successful human living consists, in order to choose the right actions; and they need this moral knowledge, to repeat, whether they are alone on a desert island or living in a community.

II. The Ethical Foundation of the Catholic Bishops' Moral Vision

The Catholic Bishops regard human personhood as sacred and hold that the institutions that make up the economy are to be judged by how well they serve the human person. They state: *"The dignity of the human person, realized in community with others, is the criterion against which all aspects of economic life must be measured."*[12] Human beings are not to be treated as merely means for some economic end. They are to be treated in ways that respect their human dignity. The notion of human dignity is, therefore, crucial in the Catholic Bishops' moral vision. Yet, what is human dignity? What does it involve, and do the duties and rights claimed by the Catholic Bishops flow from it? Regarding the first question, the Catholic Bishops note that the dignity of human beings is manifest in their "ability to reason and understand, in their freedom to shape their own lives and the life of their communities, and in the capacity for love and friendship."[13] However, exactly how does the ability to reason, choose, and care for others manifest human dignity? What is the connection? The idea here is very complex and has a long and continuing philosophical life, but it is basically this: because human beings have the capacity for human development— not only reason but will and emotion as well—they are moral agents. This is to say that they are responsible for their actions and thus merit either praise or blame for the actions they choose. The purpose or end of the choices that constitute a person's life is human fulfillment or flourishing.[14] Human fulfillment or flourishing is the standard in terms of which we determine what is morally good or bad for people.[15] Human dignity results from the fact that human beings are moral agents whose purpose is to choose the actions that will allow them to flourish and, as such, do not need to obtain their moral worth from anything else. Human dignity just is the fact that human beings are *potential* ends-in-themselves who cannot be *actual* ends-in-themselves[16] save through their own *self-directed* behavior. Human dignity requires that human beings not be used for some other project than the one they naturally have and, accordingly, human beings are entitled to be treated in certain ways. As a result, human beings have certain duties and rights.

Throughout the *Economic Pastoral*, the Catholic Bishops appeal to human fulfillment or flourishing (which can be described as a process of self-realization or self-actualization) in order to explain the moral demands of human dignity. Regarding the obligation to love others, they contend that this duty points out "the path toward true human fulfillment and happiness."[17] Regarding work, they hold that it should enable the person "to become 'more a human being,' more capable of acting intelligently, freely and in a way that leads to self-realization,"[18] and they claim that the Greek and Roman description of man as a "social animal" shows that "human beings cannot grow to full self-realization in isolation, but in interaction with others."[19] Clearly, the belief that human beings have the natural function or purpose of flourishing is the normative foundation for the Catholic Bishops understanding of human dignity. This is, of course, a most controversial assumption, but since the *Economic Pastoral* is not an essay on the foundations of normative theory, it seems only fair to work within the confines of this assumption and to examine the question of whether or not the duties and rights claimed by the Catholic Bishops do indeed flow from the dignity humans possess as a result of having the natural function or purpose of flourishing. Further, it will be especially important to examine the relationship between human flourishing and human dignity in greater detail.

III. The Catholic Bishops' Argument for Human Rights

The reasoning behind the Catholic Bishops' argument is straightforward. Given that human beings have the natural function or purpose of flourishing and that this is the standard for determining what is good or evil, certain forms of conduct are appropriate or right for human beings and certain forms of conduct are not. And given that good is to be done and evil avoided,[20] human beings have the obligation to conduct themselves appropriately. Human beings should conduct themselves in ways that are right for them as human beings, and being just is one of the appropriate ways human beings should conduct themselves. The Catholic Bishops understand justice to consist in giving others their due, and justice presupposes that some form of conduct toward others is appropriate, right for, *due* them. Yet, in order for some form of conduct to be due a person by others, there must be a basis for saying that something is due the person. Accordingly, the Catholic Bishops believe that an individual's due is broadly determined by what is necessary for the attainment of human fulfillment or flourishing. The crucial question, then, is what do the Catholic Bishops understand a person's due to be? What are the demands of justice?

Though the Catholic Bishops recognize that human beings are individuals and not merely parts of some social whole, they also recognize that human beings are social beings and, accordingly, that justice is multidimensional. The Catholic Bishops recognize three dimensions to basic justice: commutative, social, and distributive. Commutative justice concerns the relations of individuals to individuals. Social justice concerns the relations of individuals to the community, and distributive justice concerns the relations of the community to individuals. According to the Catholic Bishops, the respective demands of commutative, social, and distributive justice are these:

(a) there should be "fundamental fairness in all agreements and exchanges between individuals and private social groups";[21]

(b) "persons have an obligation to be active and productive participants in the life of society and...society has a duty to enable them to participate in this way";[22] and

(c) "the allocation of income, wealth and power in society [should] be evaluated in light of its effects on persons whose basic material needs are unmet."[23]

These are the duties or obligations imposed on individuals and on society by the requirements of basic justice. Yet, things are not as simple as they appear; for there are degrees and grades of obligation. There are demands of justice that are morally and legally binding, and demands of justice that are only morally binding. For example, one can have an obligation to keep the terms of a contract and an obligation not to tell a lie. The first type of obligation is different from, stricter than the latter. One can be compelled to fulfill the first type of obligation, while the latter depends only on one's own commitment to do the right thing.[24] What demands of justice are, according to the Catholic Bishops, legally binding, and what is the criterion they use for determining this?

The Catholic Bishops' answer to these questions is found in their claim that these demands of basic justice can be spelled out in greater detail in the human rights of every person. They thus affirm a doctrine of human rights. Further, they claim that economic rights are included in these human rights. As I noted earlier, they hold that each and every human being is entitled to life, food, clothing, shelter, rest, medical care, education, employment, healthful working conditions, and fair wages, and that these are the basic minimum conditions that the economic institutions of a society must meet. "Any denial of these rights harms persons and wounds the human community."[25] Quoting *Vatican II*, which describes the common good as "the sum of those conditions of social life which allow social groups and their individual members relatively thorough and ready access to their own fulfillment,"[26] the Catholic Bishops claim that the economic rights are included among those conditions of social life that constitute the common good and that "*the common good demands justice for all, the protection of the human rights of all.*"[27] Clearly, the demands of basic justice are expressed for the Catholic Bishops by a doctrine of human rights.

The Catholic Bishops are doing nothing new in affirming a doctrine of human rights. Pope John XXIII, in *Pacem in Terris* in 1963, explicitly enunciated such a doctrine:

> We see that every human being has the right to life, to bodily integrity, and to the means that are suitable to the proper development of life; these are primarily food, clothing, shelter, rest, medical care, and finally the necessary social services.[28]

A human rights doctrine is an official Catholic teaching.

It is important to understand that the Catholic Bishops are not merely claiming that it is right for human beings to have life, food, clothing, shelter, and so forth—the adjectival sense of 'right'—they are also claiming that having life, food, clothing, shelter, and so forth are rights—the substantive sense of 'right.' When 'right' is used in the substantive sense, it does not mean merely that it is objectively right for human beings to have life, food, clothing, shelter, and so forth. It also entails an additional claim—a moral claim that imposes an obligation or duty on others that is, if need be, legally enforceable. As the Catholic Bishops note, "*It is government's role to guarantee the minimum conditions that make...rich social activity possible, namely human rights and justice.*"[29] Thus, the demands of justice which are legally binding are those which constitute a human right; for the Catholic Bishops, all the previously mentioned human rights are legally enforceable.

IV. Arguing from Duties to Rights: A Problem

The Catholic Bishops hold that it is the duty of each and every human being to love his neighbor, to act justly, and to care for the poor. This claim is based on what they understand human flourishing to require. They further hold that "corresponding to these duties are the human rights of every person,"[30] and, as I pointed out above, these human rights include various economic rights. Ignoring for the time being certain ambiguities and peculiarities[31] in the Catholic Bishops' account of human flourishing, there is just on the face of it a problem with their argument for human rights. Their argument assumes a logical correlativity between duties and rights. Specifically, it assumes that if Smith has a duty to Jones to do X (where X is either an action or a forebearance from an action), then Jones has a right to Smith's so doing. Yet, if we understand "duty" to be *any* moral obligation, and not obligations which are morally required because of contracts or agreements voluntarily made,[32] it does not follow that Jones has such a right. One can claim, for example, "I ought to help the poor" or "It is right that I help the poor," without thereby also claiming, "The poor have a right to my help." The former statements do not in and of themselves imply the latter statement.[33] Further, rights claims are much stronger moral claims than duty claims; for rights determine what matters of morality are also to be matters of law, and unless one assumes that all moral matters should be legislated, one cannot logically move from one person's having a duty to some other to the latter having a right against the former. The Catholic Bishops are unjustified in claiming that human rights correspond to the duties they believe human flourishing requires of people.

Possibly, the Catholic Bishops do not really mean to give human rights the function of determining what matters of morality will be matters of law. That possibility will be considered later. Yet, the essential thrust of the *Economic Pastoral* is that human beings have economic rights and that these should be used in determining what policies the government of this nation should undertake. The Catholic Bishops have enunciated a doctrine of economic rights precisely in order to draw attention to some very real problems, and it is therefore incumbent on anyone who considers these problems worthy of attention to seriously consider and analyze the theory of economic rights the Catholic Bishops propound. Further, the belief in economic rights is a popular one,[34] so it seems only fair that this view of human rights be further considered and then compared to an opposing view of human rights.

V. Classification of Rights

The human rights affirmed by the Catholic Bishops are general rights as opposed to special rights. They are rights that are possessed by *all* human beings and are not due to any specific reason or circumstances. For example, Smith has the right to play golf at the country club because he is a dues-paying member, but Jones, who has not paid his dues, does not have such a right. Or the children of Jones have a right to parental care from Jones, but they do not have such a right from Smith because he is not their father. The rights proclaimed by the Catholic Bishops are not due to any special relation to another person; rather, they exist simply because someone is a human being.

The rights asserted to exist by the Catholic Bishops are moral rights as opposed to legal rights. They are rights that are used to morally evaluate legal systems and are not necessarily the rights of the legal system of some particular state or country. For example, we might say that you ought to have a legal right to criticize the government of some nation (whether or not you do in fact) because you have the moral right to do so; or, as the Catholic Bishops are claiming, people ought to have a legal right to food, clothing, shelter, and so forth because people have a moral right to them. The rights championed by the Catholic Bishops are not descriptions of the rights of some nation's legal system. Rather, they are moral claims that are used to determine what matters of morality (what ought to be) are to be matters of legality (what must be); that is, they morally determine what is to be a legal right.

The economic rights for which the Catholic Bishops argue are positive as opposed to negative rights. They are rights that impose a positive duty as opposed to a negative duty on others. All rights impose duties.[35] If Smith has a right, other people must have a duty, but it is the nature of the duty that others have that determines whether Smith's right is positive or negative. Others are subject to a positive duty with respect to Smith if and only if they are morally bound to provide Smith with some good or service. Others are subject to a negative duty with respect to Smith if and only if they are morally bound *not* to deprive Smith of some good or morally bound *not* to inflict some treatment on Smith.[36] For example, if Smith has a positive right to food, then others have the duty to provide Smith with food or the means by which Smith can obtain food. If Smith has a negative right to food, then others have the duty not to take Smith's food or the means by which he obtains food from him. In arguing for economic rights, then, the Catholic Bishops are championing a doctrine of positive human rights, because they claim that society (i.e., other people) must insure that each person has adequate food, clothing, shelter, and so forth, or the means to obtain them.

Whether the positive human rights proclaimed by the Catholic Bishops are absolute is a very important question. Yet, an examination of this question will be postponed until we have considered and developed the competing view of negative human rights. The question of whether human rights are absolute is a question faced by a negative human rights theory as well as a positive human rights theory.

VI. The Catholic Bishops Reject Negative Human Rights

Positive human rights and negative human rights are not compatible. For example, Smith's negative right to be left alone, to use his time and resources as he sees fit in a manner consistent with the negative rights of others, conflicts with the positive right of Jones to Smith's assistance. Smith's negative right to use his time and resources as he sees fit cannot be legally enforced if Jones's positive right to Smith's assistance is legally enforced. The negative, legally enforceable duty of Jones not to interfere with Smith's choices of how to use his time and resources is not compatible with the positive, legally enforceable duty of Smith to provide Jones with some of his time and resources.

The positive human rights affirmed by the Catholic Bishops require that the existence of negative human rights be denied. The positive, enforceable duty to provide food, clothing, shelter, and so forth, overrides any claim to use one's time and resources according to one's own judgments. It requires that if these duties to others are not fulfilled, then one be legally compelled to provide one's time and resources to others. The Catholic Bishops state:

> *The fulfillment of the basic needs of the poor is of the highest priority....*[And] meeting fundamental human needs must come before the fulfillment of desires for luxury consumer goods, for profits not conducive to the common good and for unnecessary military hardware.[37]

The Catholic Bishops are, of course, only reaffirming what is official Catholic teaching. As stated in *Populorum Progressio*:

It is well known how strong were the words used by the fathers of the church to describe the proper attitude of persons who possess anything toward persons in need. To quote St. Ambrose: "You are not making a gift of your possessions to the poor person. You are handing over to him what is his. For what has been given in common for the use of all, you have arrogated to yourself. The world is given to all, and not only to the rich." That is, private property does not constitute an absolute and unconditional right. No one is justified in keeping for his exclusive use what he does not need, when others lack necessities."[38]

Clearly, there can be no such thing as negative human rights according to official Catholic teaching; for the exercise of one's judgment on how to use one's time and resources is not to be legally protected—one is entitled to have the exercise of one's judgment regarding the use of time and resources protected only to the extent that such activities are for what one needs and not for luxuries. The rest of one's time and resources belong to those in need.

It might seem that the conclusion of the last paragraph is too sweeping. All the argument appears to show is that Catholic teaching does not recognize the negative right of using one's time and resources according to one's own judgments, and this does not seem to preclude Catholic teaching from recognizing other negative rights, e.g., freedom of speech or worship. Indeed, the Catholic Bishops state: "Freedom of worship and of speech are negative immunities from interference that imply self-restraint on the part of both other persons and the government."[39] Yet, if one's time and resources may be forcibly taken and used to fulfill the positive rights of those in need, why may not one be drafted to perform certain speech acts for those in need, e.g., compelling certain country and rock singers to perform at concerts whose proceeds will go to assist bankrupt Iowa farmers and starving Ethiopians?[40] In the theory of negative rights that will be sketched in the next section, the right to live one's life according to one's own choices (which is understood as entailing the right to use one's time and resources according to one's own judgments) is accorded a fundamental place in the logical structure of the theory and is hence a basic, as opposed to a derivative, right. If the Catholic Bishops' commitment to positive rights requires rejecting this basic negative right, then all other derivative rights, which would include freedom of speech, must also be rejected. Clearly, the Catholic Bishops would never endorse such a violation of the freedom of speech, but just why would they be morally precluded from doing so, given their commitment to positive rights? What is the relationship between positive and negative rights for the Catholic Bishops? Are some rights more basic or fundamental than others and, if not, how are conflicts between positive and negative rights to be resolved? The Catholic Bishops do not directly address these questions, but it is important that anyone who advances a positive theory of rights do so. Some aspects of these questions will be considered later when the concept of the "common good" is examined.

VII. An Argument for Negative Human Rights

Though usually associated with the view that human beings were once in a state of nature and formed a society by means of a "social contract," the belief that there are negative human rights does not require such assumptions[41] and can be argued for on the same normative foundation as that used by the Catholic Bishops—viz., that the natural function or purpose of a human being is human fulfillment or flourishing.[42] A comprehensive and detailed argument for negative human rights cannot, of course, be presented within the confines of this essay, but the central idea behind this view of rights can: just as human flourishing is the ultimate end or value of all human choices, so must it be that individual human beings exercising their own choices (and not those of others) while engaging in the concrete activities that constitute their lives among others is of ultimate value. Human flourishing is an activity that cannot exist unless it is the result of a person's own efforts.

The relationship between self-directedness or autonomy and human flourishing is, however, even more intimate and vital than it first appears. Self-directedness or autonomy is not merely a necessary and instrumental good. Rather, it is an inherent constituent of human flourishing. As Eric Mack notes:

> The centrality of autonomy, as a property necessary to any activity's being *constitutive* of living well, allows us to be more specific about the (proper) function of a person's activities, capacities, etc. It is the (proper) function of a person's activities, capacities, etc. to be employed *by that person* in (toward the end of) his living well. The function of a person's activities, etc. is individualized not only with regard to whose well-being it is the end of the activity (capacity, etc.) to serve but also with regard to who must employ the activity (capacity, etc.) for it to fulfill its function. The activity (capacities, etc.) of A must be employed by A if it is to fulfill its function of contributing to the active, ongoing, process of A's living well. (And A's activites, capacities, etc. have no "higher" end.)[43]

In order for us to flourish as human beings, our needs must be satisfied in a certain manner. Human needs (human potentialities) have to be satisfied (actualized) by actions that are initiated and maintained by the person himself. There is no human activity that is proper for us as human beings that does not involve autonomy or self-directedness.

If a human being were attached to a machine which satisfied his every need and thus made it possible for him not to have to do anything, this would not constitute a worthwhile human life. Human flourishing does not merely require that a human being possess, for example, health, wealth, pleasure, and friendship; these goods must rather be attained through the exercise of a person's own reason and intelligence, by a human being's unique excellence—*arete*. Yet, human reason or intelligence is not automatic. Effort is required. A human being must exercise the effort to use his reason and intelligence to gain and keep the goods human flourishing requires. Human reason (or intelligence) and autonomy (or self-directedness) are not two separate faculties, but distinct aspects of the same act. Autonomy or self-directedness is the *exercise* of human reason and intelligence and, thus, pertains to the very essence of human flourishing—it makes it what it is. Therefore, if something is to be a human good, it must be an object of human valuation, and if something is going to be actually good for an individual human being, it must be the object of an individual human being's own choices and actions. Self-directedness or autonomy is, as already stated, no mere means or necessary condition for human flourishing, but the central activity of human flourishing which is, and indeed must be, present in all other activities which constitute the human good that is human flourishing.[44]

Accordingly, since human flourishing is the ultimate end or value for human beings, and since human flourishing does not exist in the abstract, there is no such thing as human flourishing separate from the activities that constitute the flourishing of individual human beings. Human flourishing can only exist in the *self*-actualizing activities of individual human beings, and to that extent one may say that actions taken by a human being that self-actualize are actions that are ends-in-themselves. They serve no higher moral purpose. When these actions constitute the individual human being—specifically, when these actions result from principles (virtues) which constitute his character—then, the individual human being is an end-in-himself.

Each and every human being is potentially an end-in-himself who cannot be an end-in-himself save through his own self-initiated and self-maintained actions. In effect, a person must earn this status. Being an end-in-himself, like every other aspect of morality, is something that must be accomplished by the individual human being and is something for which he alone is responsible.

Immanuel Kant, the great philosopher of the German Enlightenment, claimed that one should "act in such a way that you always treat humanity, whether in your person or in the person of any other, never simply as a means, but always at the same time as an end."[45] This claim has, of course, been subject to skepticism and confusion; for not only has it never been clear just how it might be justified, it has also never been clear what exactly Kant meant by it.[46] The connection between autonomy and human flourishing sketched in the previous paragraphs provides the beginning of a clearer meaning and justification of this claim. Yet, in order to better understand the meaning and justification of Kant's claim, some additional observations about self-directedness or autonomy are necessary.

First, it must be understood that autonomy does not in and of itself guarantee that a human being will take the right actions or pursue the proper goals. To describe a person as autonomous does not necessarily mean that he is flourishing. All that autonomy or self-directedness guarantees is that a human being will be using his own reason and intelligence in determining what ends to pursue or what principles to follow.

Second, even though autonomy does not guarantee that a person is living as he should, it is nonetheless important for morality. Autonomy guarantees the fundamentally essential humanity of the person—viz., the exercise by the person of his own judgment and choice. If a human being were not autonomous, then he could be neither praised nor blamed. His actions would not be his own.

Third, autonomy also preserves the possibility that others can deal with a person in a manner that respects his humanity. Since a self-directed person is living by the exercise of his own thought and judgment, he is open to reason. He can be dealt with as a being to whom reasons can be given for why he ought or ought not to do something. A self-directed person may, of course, not find the reasons offered for why something ought or ought not to be done adequate, and he may or may not be correct in his evaluation of the reasons given. Yet, he is living as a human being—as a creature to whom reasons can make a difference, not merely as a creature who is caused to act by this or that desire.

Fourth, autonomy is an inherent power in the individual human being. One does not choose to be autonomous; rather, choice *is* autonomy. One can, of course, exercise self-directedness or fail to do so, but it is not something that others can provide.

Fifth, even though autonomy does not guarantee that a person is flourishing, self-directedness is nonetheless human flourishing described without the specific virtues called for by human rationality or the concrete goods a particular human being's reason or intelligence tells him he needs because of the specific circumstances in which he finds himself. Fundamentally speaking, human flourishing is an activity, not a static state, and an individual human being directing and using his own mind to take action to achieve ends—simply put, living according to his own choices—is the activity of human flourishing viewed most universally and abstractly.

From what we know about human flourishing, together with the foregoing comments about autonomy, we may conclude that if, for example, a person fails to develop integrity or refuses to seek friendships, or if he abdicates the responsibility of controlling and using his desires or engaging in productive work, or if he cares nothing about reason at all, then he is misusing himself, acting contrary to his natural end, and treating himself simply as a means.[47] If other persons use a person for purposes he has not chosen, regardless of what these purposes are, then the person is being misused, his natural end is not achieved, and he is being treated simply as a means.

In order to achieve a better understanding of Kant's claim, as well as the importance of a theory of negative human rights, it should be noted that only certain specific actions by a person constitute a misuse of himself, but *any* use of a person by another person which prevents him from using himself (viz., which does not allow self-directedness or autonomy) is a misuse of him.[48] Neither can the natural end of a human being, human flourishing, be achieved nor a human being treated as a being with a potential to be an end-in-himself if his autonomy is not respected. In other words, specific choices that a person makes may or may not be right for him, but whenever a person is compelled by others to follow their choices (and not his own), it is not right for him and necessarily conflicts with the natural function or purpose of a human being.

We might be tempted to say that a person can be compelled to do what is in fact good for him, but this is an error. Such a statement reifies "good"—viz., it treats the abstraction "good" as if it were a reality apart from the choices and actions of a human being.[49] If the previous account of human flourishing is correct, someone cannot be good or take the right action if he has not chosen to do this himself. Putting the matter a little differently, a world in which human beings are self-directed but fail to do the morally proper thing is better than a world in which human beings are prevented from being self-directed but "whose" actions conform to what would be right *if* they had chosen those actions themselves. Nor can a world which compels people to do the "right" thing be viewed as a morally justifiable means to creating a world in which human beings *choose* the right thing; for it is the *individual* human being's self-initiated and self-maintained achievement of his individuative and generic potentialities that is the

moral standard employed here and not some reified or collectivized version of human flourishing. A world which fails to respect the autonomy or
self-directedness of a person is a world that denies that the individual
human being is a potential end-in-himself. It is a world that fails to respect
what is fundamentally essential about a person's humanity, and it is a world
that fails to grant him what is fundamentally his due.[50]

As I said earlier, a comprehensive and detailed argument for negative
human rights cannot be given here, but the foregoing considerations do
lead to a doctrine of negative human rights. As long as it is possible for one
to live in a community of persons who can exercise control over what they
do, it can never be morally justifiable to use people for purposes to which
they have not consented. This moral principle is, however, not as simple as
it first appears, and it is more fully expressed in the claim that individual
human beings have basic natural rights to life, liberty, and property. These
are negative rights. These rights are, however, like the rights advocated by
the Catholic Bishops, in that they are general rights—they apply to all
human persons and are not due to any special relation between persons—
and they are moral rights—they are used to determine what legal rights
there should be. According to this theory of negative human rights, the
right to life means "the right to engage in self-sustaining and self-generated
action—which means: the freedom to take all the actions required by the
nature of a rational being for the support, the furtherance, the fulfillment
and the enjoyment of his own life."[51] The right to life is thus interpreted
maximally as the right to live your life according to your own choices and
entails the right to liberty—viz., the right to conduct your life free from the
initiatory use or threat of physical compulsion, coercion, or interference
from others.

The right to life maximally interpreted also entails the right to property.
As John Hospers has said:

> The *right to property* is a special case of the right to life in its maximal
> sense: you have the right to live by your voluntary choices, and among
> those decisions are the ones to earn and buy things you can call your own.
> The importance of the right to own things can hardly be overestimated. If
> human beings were incorporeal spirits, they would not need possessions;
> but since human beings live in the material world, they need food and
> shelter in order to survive. Moreover, they can prosper only if they can
> plan their lives long range—for example, by working and saving for the
> future—but they can't do this if there is nothing to rely on as their own.[52]

In fact, unless a person's life is confined to the person's outer epidermic
layer, the nonconsensual use of a person's property—whether it be schol-
arly books, business enterprises, or income—is a direct attack on the per-

son. One cannot divorce what one has produced from one's personhood without reducing the human person to an atomistic existence.

Simply put, these basic natural rights require that people not murder, assault, kidnap, and steal from each other. These duties are basic and are legally enforceable. Any positive rights that exist are derivative. That is to say, they are special rights which flow from an exercise of the basic negative rights to life, liberty, and property, e.g., my right to medical care flows from my basic negative right to act freely and to choose to enter a contract to obtain medical care. Such a positive right, deriving as it does from basic negative rights, is legally protected. Besides deriving from a contract, positive rights can also result from relationships voluntarily created, e.g., the decision to have children. The positive rights of children and the corresponding duties of parents to children are also legally enforceable. Yet, the most important positive rights for this theory of negative human rights are the civil and political rights of citizens of a free society.

> Citizens, upon having established and/or consented to live under a government which exists so as to protect their basic rights, owe their government certain (agreed upon) duties—payments for services, participation in administration, cooperation in crime detection and prevention, offering testimony in pursuit of justice, etc.[53]

Though certainly not as great in number as the Catholic Bishops would wish to affirm, these positive rights and duties are by no means negligible. Further, there is nothing in the negative human rights theory that precludes the creation of numerous positive rights and duties. All that is required is that the subsequent positive rights and duties not contradict the basic negative rights to life, liberty, and property.

In order to finish this sketch of negative human rights, one remaining point needs to be made. The basic negative rights and derivative positive rights affirmed by the negative rights theorist do not by any means exhaust the moral realm. In exercising their rights persons can most assuredly do things that are not right—not right for themselves and not right for others. A negative rights theorist would by no means wish to deny that there are many obligations that persons have to self and others that are important and vital for human living, even though they should not be legally enforced. Making moral judgments and acting on the basis of them are not only an exercise of basic negative rights, they are obligations that everyone has. Passing moral judgments on the behavior of others and exhorting them to change their ways—what is sometimes today called "imposing" your values on others—are many times morally required and nothing to which the negative rights theory sketched above would object. The scope of moral obligations is much wider than the scope of legal obligations.

VIII. Positive Versus Negative Rights

It is time to compare these two competing theories of basic human rights. They both claim to be theories of natural rights, and they both presuppose that human beings have the natural function or purpose of human flourishing.[54] The rights that both theories claim are more than mere "powers" that human beings have; rather, they are based on a consideration of what is objectively right for human beings. The argument for positive human rights holds that having life, food, clothing, shelter, rest, medical care, education, healthful working conditions, and fair wages are authentic human goods. It is objectively right for every human being to have these, and thus every human being has a right to these. The argument for negative human rights claims that living according to your own choices is an authentic human good. It is objectively right for human beings to live this way, and thus every human being has a right to live in this manner. Stated in this way, it is hard to see which account of human rights is more plausible. Life, food, clothing, shelter, and so forth are certainly necessary for human flourishing, but so is living according to one's own choices. It might, however, seem that the former are more important to human flourishing; for it is very hard to live according to your own choices if you do not have sufficient amounts of food, clothing, and shelter. This is, of course, true. Yet, this observation ignores what differentiates human living from other forms of animal life. The natural function or purpose of a human being is not mere survival. It is to live well or flourish, but human flourishing is not, as I noted previously, merely having what it takes to live well. We live well or flourish as human beings only to the extent that we use our own reason and intelligence in creating, obtaining, employing, and using the needed goods of life. Yet, our reason and intelligence do not function automatically. Our reason and intelligence will only function through our own personal effort. As Henry B. Veatch has observed:

> No human being can ever be said to live well, or to live as a human being ought to live, unless it is on the basis of *his own* decisions and choices made in the light of *his own* understanding of what is best for him and what the good life demands.[55]

Self-directedness or autonomy, to repeat what was said earlier, is an inherent feature of the activities which constitute human flourishing and is not merely a means—as food, clothing, and shelter are—to human flourishing. Having the various goods and services called for by positive rights is objectively good and right for a person as a means to fulfillment, but having the liberty called for by negative rights to live according to one's own choices is objectively good and right for a human being as an essential aspect of the end that is a person's fulfillment.

Stated more exactly, food, clothing, shelter, and so forth are necessary conditions for the *existence* of human flourishing, but self-directedness or autonomy is necessary for human flourishing to be what it is. Self-directedness or autonomy pertains to the very essence of human flourishing—it makes it what it is. Specifically, autonomy makes human flourishing a "moral good," as opposed to some other kind of good; it differentiates the actualization of potentialities in a human being from those in the rest of nature—for example, an acorn becoming an oak. Thus, if the fulfillment or flourishing of the individual human being is the standard of morality, and if self-directedness or autonomy is an essential aspect of human flourishing, negative rights are more fundamental than positive rights. Negative rights seek to protect that essential feature of human flourishing that must exist if human beings are to be moral agents. As Tibor R. Machan has noted:

> Each man must be free to choose to gain the knowledge and perform the actions required for his life—i.e., if his life is to have the opportunity to be a good one, if he is to have the option between moral and immoral conduct, an option open to him by nature. The choice to learn, to judge, to evaluate, to appraise, to decide what he ought to do in order to live his life must be each person's own, otherwise he simply has no opportunity to excel or fail at the task. His moral aspirations cannot be fulfilled (or left unfulfilled) if he is not the source of his own actions, if they are imposed or forced upon him by others.[56]

Though it is true that living according to one's own choices is good and right for human beings in a way that is more fundamental than merely having one's economic needs met, it might be objected that this does not show that living according to one's own choices is a right. Rather, it only shows that *if there are any rights at all*, negative rights are more fundamental than positive rights. As presented so far, the theory of negative rights would seem just as guilty of illicitly moving from the adjectival sense of "right" to the substantive sense of "right" as the Catholic Bishops are when they argue from duties to rights in their doctrine of positive economic rights. This is an important objection, one that cannot be fully considered here, but there can, at least, be a few things said by way of meeting this objection.

Though it is right for people to be self-directed or autonomous, do people have the right—in the substantive sense—to live according to their own choices? In order to respond to this question, the structure of the argument for negative rights must be examined more closely. Since negative rights protect autonomy, and since autonomy is an essential aspect of the moral purpose of human beings, one does not determine whether protecting a person's autonomy is right by recourse to the consequences of providing such protection. One can reason this way when trying to evaluate morally a means to human flourishing, e.g., wealth and power, but one cannot reason this way when trying to evaluate morally the central feature necessary to any activity being a constituent of a human being's moral good. It is good, right for, human beings to live according to their own choices and bad, wrong for, human beings not to live according to their own choices, and we know this from our analysis of the very character of human flourishing and not from looking at the results or consequences of self-directed or autonomous actions by human beings.

As the central feature necessary to any activity being a constituent of human flourishing, the rightness of self-directedness or autonomy is due to itself, not anything else. When working at this fundamental level of analysis—when speaking of that activity which must pertain to all other activities in order for them to be right but which does not itself obtain its rightness because it contributes to some other end—you are dealing with an activity which is an end-in-itself and to which "right" applies in both an adjectival and substantive sense. Being self-directed or autonomous is a right activity because ultimately it is right in itself.

The adjectival and substantival character of the rightness of autonomy or self-directedness was expressed by Ayn Rand when she observed that "if man is to live on earth, then it is *right* for him to use his mind, it is *right* to act on his own free judgment; it is *right* to work for his values and keep the product of his work. If life on earth is his purpose, he has the *right* to live as a rational being."[57] Before we even address questions of what people should think, how they should act, or what they should do, we know that human beings ought to use their minds, act on their own judgment, and create and keep the values they produce. These activities are not, to repeat, right for human beings merely because they are necessarily conducive to human flourishing. Indeed, we can easily conceive of cases where someone uses his mind, acts on his own judgment, or pursues and keeps values in ways that are not conducive to his human well-being. Rather, these activities are right because they are the central necessary features of human flourishing and as such are right activities in themselves. They are right in the adjectival sense because they are right in the substantival sense. No matter what ends a person may choose or how he may go about achieving those ends, it is both right and a right that he choose and pursue ends.[58]

It is the very fact that a human being's moral purpose is human flourishing which shows that a person is justified in living according to his own choices for his own well-being and that others are unjustified in preventing this. Others are unjustified in bringing it about that a person's activities are not self-directed because of the fact that being self-directed is an essential aspect of that which is an end-in-itself, viz., flourishing of individual human beings. The very moral principle that others must invoke to justify their pursuit of their own flourishing, as compared to some other moral principle (e.g., the greatest good for the greatest number), shows they would be unjustified in using others for purposes to which they have not consented. A person has a moral claim against others bringing it about that his activities are directed by others in virtue of being a potential end-in-himself who cannot be an end-in-himself save through his own self-directed behavior.[58]

Yet, this response still does not entirely answer the question: for why is the duty not to use persons for purposes they have not chosen an enforceable duty? The answer to this question also rests on the connection between autonomy and flourishing. If the foregoing account of human flourishing is correct, we know that protecting the self-directedness or autonomy of the human person is the primary condition for human life among others—i.e., it is that condition which must exist before anything else—if we are to have *self*-actualizing human beings. By the same token, we know that those who compel others to act against their own judgment or expropriate the fruits of their labor make a morally fulfilling human life for others impossible. To the extent that such acts of violence and coercion characterize a human community, a morally decent human community becomes impossible. Thus, the use of force against those who initiate it is morally justified in order to protect the primary condition for the possibility of a moral human community.

The legal enforcement of negative rights requires that other moral agents refrain from invading what Robert Nozick has called a person's "moral space."[59] The use of force is morally permitted only after a person has chosen to violate some other person's negative rights[60]—in effect, only after the person has chosen coercion as a means of interacting with others. Negative rights do not, of course, guarantee that people will choose what they should, but they do provide the political condition that will protect the moral agency of persons and thus not destroy the possibility that people will choose what they should.

The doctrine of positive rights affirmed by the Catholic Bishops does, of course, note various goods and services that human beings need in order to flourish, but nowhere do the Catholic Bishops establish that a person has a right—in the substantive sense—to these goods. Furthermore, by making the provision of these goods and services duties that others can be com-

pelled to provide, the Catholic Bishops confuse the means to human fulfillment with human fulfillment itself, and thus make having what it takes to
live well more important than living well. This, in turn, gives rise to the
belief that the lives of individual human beings may be sacrificed (usually
only in terms of time and resources, but not always) on the altar of providing for the needs of others. As a result of this confusion, positive rights
require the misuse of human beings, using people for purposes they have
not chosen, treating them as mere means and thus without human dignity.
In contrast, the view of negative rights sketched in this section holds that
the lives of individual human beings are not to be treated as resources to be
used by any person, group of persons, or government who can claim need
of them.

Possibly, the Catholic Bishops would argue that an incorrect account of
what they are demanding has been presented. They do not wish to deny the
rights to life, liberty, and property, but only to claim that these rights are
not absolute and that others have a right to a minimum of the necessities of
life. They claim that no one has the right to fulfill their desires for luxuries
while others lack basic necessities.

Yet, this response will not do. If the negative rights to life, liberty, and
property are not absolute, then are the positive rights to life, food, clothes,
shelter, and so forth absolute? If not, the notion of "rights" becomes worth-
less. The whole point of claiming a right is to say that regardless of the good
consequences that issue from doing X, if doing X violates a basic human
right, then doing X is not morally justifiable. Yet, if there are no absolute
rights, if all rights can be overriden by some other "stronger" moral claim,
then there would really be no point at all to claiming them. This is not to
say that the adjudication of rights cannot be troublesome, but it is to say
that if the notion of "rights" is to have an ethical function, then some rights
must be absolute.[61]

If, on the other hand, positive rights *are* absolute (and negative rights are
not), then there is an immediate problem. As Christopher W. Morris has
noted:

> If natural rights are positive, then individuals are obligated to provide
> others with certain goods or services (e.g., food, medical care). If these
> rights are absolute, no moral considerations can override respect for
> them. However, there may be conditions of scarcity where individuals
> cannot provide the goods in question. Assuming that "ought implies can,"
> we can have some absolute duties with which we cannot comply. But that
> is absurd.[62]

It is very difficult, to say the least, to understand an obligation that is
impossible to fulfill. The Catholic Bishops, then, face a dilemma. Either

positive rights are absolute or they are not. If they are not absolute, then the Catholic Bishops cannot justify their claim that human beings have a right (in the sense of a moral claim that "trumps" all other moral claims) to life, food, clothing, shelter, and so forth. If the positive rights are absolute, then the Catholic Bishops are committed to holding the absurd view that there can be duties which are impossible to fulfill.

This dilemma may not, however, be decisive; for it might be that the conclusion of the second horn of the dilemma does not really follow. It does not necessarily seem absurd to say that "those in need still have a moral claim on those who are not, even if in certain circumstances the need cannot be met. It serves to remind those who are not in need that they have a duty to fulfill that need."[63] Moreover, the difficulty in determining the exact sense of "can" in the "ought implies can" principle, not to mention the meaning of "absolute," should make us cautious in accepting this dilemma. Yet, the Catholic Bishops still have the burden of explaining why positive rights are absolute and negative rights are not. On the other hand, since negative rights only require moral agents to refrain from actions that violate the negative rights of others, it is a political condition that all other moral agents are capable of fulfilling. Every moral agent is capable of not choosing to coerce others to conduct themselves for purposes they have not chosen.[64] Fulfilling the conditions required by negative rights is thus easier than trying to fulfill the conditions required by positive rights. Claiming that negative rights are absolute is, however, a difficult position to defend. Surely, there seems to be times when even these rights must be violated.

Earthquakes, floods, fires, and shipwrecks appear to be the sorts of situations that people often have in mind when they consider circumstances in which negative rights ought to be violated for the benefit of all. Yet, the issue faced is one of how these situations should be described. Are such situations examples of negative rights being overruled by considerations of the common good or of situations which cannot be approached in terms of considerations appropriate to social and political life?

Negative rights theorists would claim that there are situations which morally call for the disregard of negative rights, but not their violation. The basis for this distinction is twofold. First, negative rights are the political condition that ought to exist in a community, if the well-being of each and every member is to have any possibility of being achieved. As long as it is in principle possible for every member to attain his well-being by the exercise of his negative rights, negative rights are applicable. Yet, second, there can be situations in which it is in principle impossible for everyone to pursue his well-being by the exercise of negative rights. Such situations are called "emergencies." An emergency situation is an unexpected event, usually of limited duration, which makes it impossible for every person to pursue his well-being and, at the same time, not interfere with the negative rights of others. An emergency calls for immediate action to restore normal conditions.

During the attempt to restore a normal state of affairs negative rights do not apply because it makes no sense to say that the negative rights of others ought to be respected, if the terms under which negative rights are justified, viz., the pursuit of well-being, requires that negative rights be ignored. Moreover, in an emergency there is no point in talking of the common good of the political community. The benefits of social life cannot be attained in a life-boat or in the middle of an earthquake. In such cases, it is not the common good *of* the political community that is at stake, but rather the political community itself.

However, it does not follow from the realization that political principles are not applicable in all situations that one can regard any situation one chooses as an emergency. Though there may indeed be borderline cases, negative rights theorists would contend that after the "emergency" is over, the burden of proof is on the person who claims to have disregarded negative rights only because the situation was an emergency in the sense defined above. Further, it should be noted that the attempt to expand "emergency" to include any situation where good results will ensue from ignoring the negative rights of someone ultimately deprives the term of its initial meaning, and thus causes it to lose whatever ability it had to describe a situation that poses difficulties for a theory of rights. Thus, the admission that there can be emergency situations does not imply that negative rights can be "trumped" by considerations of consequences. Finally, the claim that an emergency situation describes the fundamental state of nature in which human beings exist is subject to direct empirical refutation—consider the fortunes made by insurance companies betting against disasters.[65] Whenever and wherever political principles are applicable, negative human rights can be considered absolute.

The Catholic Bishops' basic reason for rejecting absolute negative rights seems to be expressed by the claim that the fulfillment of the basic needs of the poor is of the highest priority and must come before the fulfillment of desires for luxury consumer goods. Though the picture of two individuals, one fat from mindless gluttony, the other lean and starving in the street comes to mind, the Catholic Bishops never present the criteria for determining when one has more than he needs and is only fulfilling desires for luxuries. Are a toaster, a television set, a color television set, a color television set with remote control, a video cassette recorder, a snow blower, an automatic rear window defroster, a trip to Florida once a year luxuries which one does not have a right to keep? Certainly, compared to the situation faced by the starving people of Ethiopia, these items are luxuries. There is hardly an item in the homes of the vast majority of the citizens of the United States that is not a luxury when compared to the living conditions of the "Third World." Yet, if negative rights are not absolute and if those in need have a right to the resources of those who have more than they need to meet their minimum material needs, then these luxuries are to be foregone and the income used to purchase these luxuries redistributed to those in need. Indeed, it is most difficult to see how a philosopher who accepts the Catholic Bishops' claim that the fulfillment of the needs of the poor has highest moral priority can do anything less than stop philosophizing and begin working full time for the poor. Or would it be that a philosopher would be morally justified only if he devoted all his time urging others to help the poor?

It might be that the Catholic Bishops would wish to have such redistribution schemes only carried out *intra*nationally and not *inter*nationally—the idea being that we have a greater duty to help the poor nearest to us than those far away. Of course, the problem with this suggestion is that the poor of the United States are generally much better off than the poor of the rest of the world. Should the poor of the United States who are closer but less needy be helped first, or should the poor of the rest of the world who are more needy but farther away be helped first? Maybe they can both be helped at the same time, and perhaps this is only a problem faced on the practical level and not one that should be of concern here. Yet, no matter which way the Catholic Bishops' claim is taken, the principle is clear: "Only those who rise no higher than the barest minimum of subsistence have the *right* to material possessions."[66] This is not to say that, practically speaking, one may not be allowed to keep a large part of the income used for luxuries or that, after some consideration of the common good, it might not be deemed morally permissible for one to keep a large part of this income. Rather, it is to say that as a matter of moral principle one does not have a right to that portion of income used for luxuries and pleasures.

What is crucial here, however, is the assumption on the part of the Catholic Bishops that luxuries and pleasures are not part of a fulfilling human life. Luxuries are pointless for animals (though not necessarily their owners), and pleasures are not needed by disembodied minds. But human beings are not merely animals or disembodied minds. Human beings are different from the other animals and have the need for luxuries, and yet human beings are animals and have the need for pleasures. Luxuries and pleasures are *human* needs. Human flourishing is not mere survival, and it is objectively good and right for human beings to use their reason and intelligence to create, obtain, employ, and use luxuries and pleasures in creating a fulfilling human life for themselves. The Catholic Bishops are simply wrong to separate luxuries and pleasures from basic human needs.

There are, of course, people with large incomes who engage in drunkeness, licentiousness, and debauchery, who think more of themselves than they should, indulge every whim, and care nothing for others. Is it right that people should conduct themselves in this way when there are others starving? No. In fact, it would not be right even if there were no wealthy people and even if there were no people in need. If the Catholic Bishops' message is simply that each person should use his reason and intelligence in pursuing luxuries and pleasures, be mindful of those in need, and practice the virtues of benevolence and love, then there is no objection. Nor is it unimportant that moral authorities should urge the practice of such virtues. As I noted earlier, the negative rights theorist would hold that the moral arena is and should be wider than the legal arena.

Yet, the Catholic Bishops proclaim that people have "economic rights." These rights are inconsistent with the negative rights to life, liberty, and property, and it is on this issue that the dispute centers. Some still might maintain that this dispute is exaggerated; for the Catholic Bishops appeal to the "principle of subsidiarity" for determining the scope and limit of governmental intervention. "This principle states that in order to protect basic justice government should undertake only those initiatives which exceed the capacity of individuals or private groups acting independently."[67] Yet, the principle of subsidiarity deals with the application of human rights to society, not with the content or character of human rights, and the dispute raised in this essay concerns the Catholic Bishops' conception of basic human rights. Though some might not wish to recognize just how far the Catholic Bishops have gone in proclaiming their doctrine of positive natural rights and just how fundamentally opposed the *Economic Pastoral* is to the conception of negative natural rights upon which the moral justification of this country's revolution was based and its constitution developed,[68] it is nonetheless true that there is a clash of moral visions. Yet, determining whether a theory of positive rights or a theory of negative rights more successfully reflects the moral vision of this country's "Founding Fathers" does not determine which of the two theories, if either, is true. It is the philosophical argument that counts.

It might be argued that to the extent that someone's choices and actions are obviously wrong, he does not have a right to conduct himself in such a manner and, thus, may have that portion of his income which he uses so foolishly appropriated to promote the common good, e.g., helping the needy. As Henry B. Veatch argues:

> A person's rights to life, liberty, and property...[are] *the necessary means* of his living wisely and responsibly and of his becoming and being the person that a human being ought to be. Accordingly, to the extent to which an individual does little more than devote his life to indulging his every personal whim and inclination or to the extent to which he gives himself over to love of inordinate gain—or even suppose that he so pampers life and limb that he becomes little more than an accomplished hypochondriac, a veritable *malade imaginaire*—then there is no longer a sense in which what he does, in the exercise of his freedom, is any longer necessary to becoming the person his natural end requires that he be. The actions that he takes and the conduct that he pursues are then no longer right at all; nor can his natural right to life, liberty, and property be said to entitle him so to live in the way he has foolishly chosen to do. In other words, that one should abuse one's right must not itself be taken to be a right, or even one's right in any strict sense.[69]

Veatch is correct. The exercise of self-directedness or autonomy in the case of a person such as he describes does not lead to a good human life. *If* autonomy were only the necessary means to human flourishing, then the claim that a person has an absolute right to live according to his own choices would be groundless. Yet, Veatch and the Catholic Bishops have forgotten what has been continually stressed throughout this essay: autonomy is not merely the necessary means to human flourishing, but is of the very essence of human flourishing itself. The moral propriety of respecting an individual's autonomy is not tied to the individual's making the morally appropriate choices. It is an essential aspect of human flourishing and, as such, does not need anything else to make it right. There is, then, just no way that a human being can attain his moral good—i.e., fulfill his duties to self and others—if he is not the author of his actions, if they have been compelled by others. In the sense that was defined earlier, the negative natural rights to life, liberty, and property remain absolute. Veatch in this instance, and the Catholic Bishops more generally, cannot escape the charge that they endorse treating a human being as a mere means to be sacrificed for the common good.

IX. The Common Good

The Catholic Bishops conceive of a human being as a social and political creature. Human beings do not live as isolated individuals, but as members of a family, a social group, and a society. As I noted earlier, the demands of basic justice are, for the Catholic Bishops, not confined merely to what obligations persons owe to other persons. They also include the obligations of persons to society, and of society to persons. Basic justice has three dimensions: commutative, social, and distributive. The Catholic Bishops note that "Catholic social teaching spells out the basic demands of justice in greater detail in the human rights of every person,"[70] but their conception of human rights has been evaluated and found wanting. It might, however, seem that this evaluation has concentrated too much on the individuative features of human nature and not enough on the social. The human rights that the Catholic Bishops proclaim result from the recognition "that persons are essentially social and institution building beings."[71] Moreover, though the common good of a political community must include the basic human rights of every person, this does not mean that the common good is exhausted by these rights.[72] Thus, there might be enforceable duties that persons have to social institutions and social institutions to persons which cannot be understood merely by considering what the human flourishing of some isolated individual involves but only by considering as well the social and political character of persons. A person's well-being is, after all, connected with the rest of society. If this is so, then why may not the set of human rights affirmed by the Catholic Bishops be construed not as absolute positive rights that individuals possess, but as a bundle of rights—negative as well as positive—which result from a consideration of man's social as well as individuative features? These rights would, of course, conflict, but would be balanced and enforced by appealing to the common good of the political community.

More properly, the human rights affirmed by the Catholic Bishops would really be a list of basic human needs—personal, familial, social, economic, religious, and political—and would not function as rights in the substantive sense. They would not be principles which in themselves determine what is to be a matter of law. Roman Catholic rights theory could, then, be described as follows:

> There is no *abstract* set of structural norms which determine which group or which rights claims take priority in a given social and historical moment....The principle of subsidiarity...continues to stress the importance of claims of small and intermediate associations. The need for communal solidarity continues to call for integration of these associations in service of the common good. The developing Catholic model of social interaction is thus fundamentally a set of norms for discerning how these competing and conflicting claims are to be balanced. It is a method for ongoing exercise of political responsibilities throughout the whole of society. This responsibility falls on all individuals, groups, and classes because of their obligations to and claims on society as a whole.[73]

The balancing of the conflicting needs would be a political task to be undertaken in the light of historical and social circumstances for the purpose of attaining the common good.

According to this account, the Catholic Bishops' view of rights would be a function of a human being's social and political features just as much as his individuative ones. These rights would not be absolute and would conflict, but would ideally be balanced in the political process of trying to establish the common good of each and all. The common good is the end or goal of a human community. It is that-for-the-sake-of-which a human community exists. A final and complete definition of the common good is, however, not possible; "for no one can state with complete finality what the potentialities of the human community are."[74] The common good is, however, the standard to be used in determining what duties will be legally enforced. Assuming that this account does more or less express the Catholic Bishops' approach to human rights, what effect does this have on the criticisms that have been offered?

The answer to this question is "very little." The view of negative human rights that was sketched did not deny or fail to take cognizance of the social and political character of human beings. Though the view of man advanced was individualist in character, it was not Hobbesian; rather, it was Aristotelian or, at least, quasi-Aristotelian. In terms of his natural origins, man is not an isolated entity in a state of nature. We are always born into a society or community. Man is not an entity who initially takes it upon himself to join society. Further, man possesses certain potentialities that cannot be properly attained in isolation. Man needs association and companionship with others if he is to flourish. It is through cooperation and collaboration with others that we come to provide for our basic needs and highest aspirations. Human fulfillment or flourishing must involve life in society. Man is a social and political animal.

Yet, a human being's need for social or community life implies neither that a human being is no longer an individual entity nor that the existence of a community is not dependent on the actions of and relationships between individual human beings. Individual human beings constitute their community and serve as the foundation of its being. Human societies or communities are not entities which exist in their own right, separate and apart from the individuals who make them up. This is not to say that there cannot be human groups which possess a kind of unity which cannot be explained by the mere physical existence of the individuals who compose them. In Aristotelian terms, human groups exist as an accident of individual human substances—that is to say, they exist as the result of the shared beliefs and goals of the individual members that compose the group. As D.J. Allan states:

> Men have capacities which can only be developed to the full within the *polis*; but there is a reverse side of this, namely that the State is only as real as a community of individual men whose capacities have been thus developed. Man is a social animal in an even higher degree than the bee. But then he is also not a social animal in the same way as the bee: he possesses the power of speech, which permits, and is naturally designed for, consultation about mutual advantage.[75]

A human group is a moral entity, not a substance or "organic" whole. Its unity results only from its members judging that common action is needed to attain an end and deciding to pursue that end.

The fact that human beings are social and political animals and thus need others in order to attain greater knowledge and material well-being, not to mention love and friendship, does not in any way make the attainment of human flourishing any less something the individual human being must do for himself. One can be told truths, endowed with wealth, and given affection: but possessing these does not constitute fulfillment—a person must still use his intelligence and ability to choose to fashion a worthwhile existence. Membership in a society or community does not remove the necessary connection between self-fulfillment and individual responsibility. Our fundamental need for social and political life does not come from what we can receive *from* others but, rather, from what we can do *with* others. It is the greater possibility for growth and achievement that social and political life affords that constitutes its extreme importance for human beings. Community life does not change the need to be the author of one's own action, it intensifies it.

If the function of government for the Catholic Bishops is the promotion of the common good of the political community, then the notion of the common good must be examined carefully. Since the political community is not an entity in its own right, there can be no good for it *as such*. The political common good is an intermediate end which is designed to serve the well-being of all members of the community. Yet, this does not mean that the common good is simply the greatest good for the greatest number, or even the sum total of all individual, personal goods. Rather, the common good of the political community is that general condition which exists in the community so as to allow for the possibility that each and every human being may flourish.

Accordingly, the common good of the political community is not a determinate end—it is not the object of a human purpose with identifiable characteristics which can be used to help specify appropriate and inappropriate courses of action for the realization of that end. Instead, the common good of the political community is a procedural end—it is the object of a human purpose the function of which is to define the conditions under which the pursuit of other (determinate) ends will occur.[76] Thus, when we speak of the common good of a society like the United States, it is not to be thought of as a determinate end. A political community is not a human group like a basketball team or an orchestra; for there is no single, determinate end that every citizen of the United States has decided to pursue. There is not even one determinate conception of human flourishing held by all the citizens of the United States.[77] Whatever is claimed to belong to the common good of the political community must be something which is procedural and in that way good for each and every member of the political community.

Since the requirements of human fulfillment are determined by the nature of a human being, and since this must be understood as applying to every human being—past, present, and future—the moral good for a human being has to be defined in terms of abstract principles covering a wide variety of concretes.

> It is up to every individual to apply these principles to the particular goals and problems of his own life. It is only principles that can provide a proper common bond among all men; men can agree on a principle without necessarily agreeing on the choice of concretes. For instance men can agree that one should work, without prescribing any man's particular choice of work.

> It is only with abstract principles that a social system may properly be concerned. A social system cannot force a particular good on a man nor can it force him to seek the good: it can only maintain conditions of existence which leave him free to seek it. A government cannot live a man's life, it can only protect his freedom. It cannot prescribe concretes, it cannot tell him how to work, what to produce, what to buy, what to say, what to write, what values to seek—what form of happiness to pursue—it can only uphold the principle of his right to make such choices.

> It is in this sense that "the common good"...lies not in *what* men do when they are free, but in the fact *that* they are free.[78]

There is a difference between treating abstract moral principles as extensions of the lives and choices of individuals—where individuals are the fundamental realities and adherence to principles is a guide to successful living—and the reification of abstractions—where the abstractions take on an existence of their own and individuals are treated as mere place-holders or receptacles for the abstract moral principles.[79] Conceptions of the common good of the political community must be careful not to reify that common good into something that members of the political community "receive." A legal system whose constitution is founded on negative human rights provides for a conception of the common good that is procedural. Such a legal system would neither be guilty of reifying the common good nor reducing the common good to merely a sum of individual, personal goods.

The theory of negative human rights previously sketched and used to criticize the Catholic Bishops' theory of economic rights does not ignore the social character of human beings and does not commit itself to some kind of atomism. Yet, it might still be argued that a determinate conception of the common good is necessary in order to provide for social unity and community spirit. The Catholic Bishops are, of course, correct to note that without a sense of community, the very principles which provide the foundation of our society will be forgotten and the existence of this society threatened. But a determinate end is not consistent with a society as diverse and large as the United States. Further, there is nothing about a procedural conception of the common good that would preclude social unity and community spirit. As Douglas J. Den Uyl has observed:

> If this sense of community is not to be an empty ideal, the common bond must be something that *can* be shared by a pluralistic society. The most likely candidate here is a common commitment to a set of procedural principles that promote diversity and encourage individual achievement. There is nothing in the nature of such principles that precludes a common commitment to them accompanied by a communal or shared sense of their worth and value. Indeed, a shared sense of commitment to the protection of individual (negative) rights is vital to their maintenance, since that sense of commitment helps in the protection of those rights and keeps those in power from expropriating them.[80]

If the positive rights affirmed by the Catholic Bishops are not absolute, then there is a question that seems particularly troubling: What normative criteria will be used to guide the political process in determining whose basic needs are to be legally provided for? Granted that the method used to determine such criteria is supposed to be a dynamic one and must consider historical and social circumstances, what guidance beyond the "principle of subsidiarity" and appeals to "human dignity" do the Catholic Bishops offer to the politician? The Catholic Bishops provide a laundry list of human needs, and even duties, but what normative criteria do they provide for deciding what will become a matter for the coercive authority of government? The common good of the political community is the traditional answer from Roman Catholic moral theory, but this notion is notoriously difficult to understand, let alone justify. Beyond a procedural conception of the common good which is specified by a theory of negative rights, the common good of the political community is either a reified abstraction or an empty ideal.[81] Yet, the Catholic Bishops reject a theory of absolute negative rights. So, what help can be offered regarding this question? The Catholic Bishops state:

> Our approach in analyzing the U.S. economy is pragmatic and evolution-ary in nature. We live in a "mixed" economic system which is a product of a long history of reform and adjustment. It is in the spirit of this American pragmatic tradition of reform that we seek to continue the search for a more just economy.[82]

Yet, as Socrates asked, "What is justice?"[83] and as the citizens of this country ask, "Is there anything more than the majority vote of politicians[84] that will protect our life, liberty, and property?"

X. The Free Market

The Catholic Bishops note that Roman Catholic teaching "rejects the notion that a free market automatically produces justice."[85] Now there is a sense in which the statement "a free market automatically produces jus-tice" is true, and a sense in which it is false. Before dealing with this statement, however, the exact nature of a free market should be made clear and differentiated from the current American economic system.

The term 'free market' is not solely descriptive. It describes a set of economic and social arrangements that presupposes a certain ethical per-spective. For example, Murder Incorporated would not be regarded as a business firm in the free market, but would instead be viewed as something criminal which ought not and must not be allowed to operate. Further, the term 'profit' does not merely mean a return on an economic exchange that is above costs; it also involves a certain type of exchange—namely, a free or voluntary exchange. In order to understand the exact meaning of these terms, we must take recourse to the ethical perspective which underlies their meaning.

The free market is an economic and social system that is based on the recognition of individual rights or, as they have been described in this essay, basic negative human rights. These rights are rights to actions—the right to take all the actions necessary for the support and furtherance of one's life, and the right to the action of producing or earning something and keeping, using, and disposing of it according to one's goals. To have a right in this sense morally obligates others to abstain from physical compulsion, coercion, or interference, or the threat thereof. Such action may be taken only in self-defense and only against those who have initiated physical compulsion or coercion. To have these rights morally sanctions the freedom to act by means of one's voluntary, uncoerced choice for one's own goals.[86] The activities of producing and exchanging goods and services in a free market is, then, both protected and governed by this conception of individual rights.

It should be clear that the current American economic system is not protected or governed by the foregoing conception of individual rights. The status quo is, as the Catholic Bishops have noted, a "mixed" economic system. There are subsidies, tariffs, quotas, manipulations of the money supply, government promoted and licensed monopolies, and myriad forms of regulations, and while the government does have an important role in legally implementing individual rights,[87] the vast majority of government's activities in the marketplace today constitute a violation of individual rights and a continuing erosion of what remains of a free market. Thus, when the Catholic Bishops decry the unemployment rate for minority teenagers, the economic devastation of the American family farm, and the millions of people in poverty, there are some important questions to be asked: Are these problems the result of the free market, or are they the result of years of governmental intervention? And if the problems are not due to governmental intervention, would calling for government action which violates individual rights solve the problems? Answering these questions for each of the aforementioned problems is far beyond the scope of this essay. Nowhere in the *Economic Pastoral* do the Catholic Bishops consider the possibility that the problems they speak of might result from policies that violate individual rights and destroy the workings of the free market. Yet, there are numerous studies that argue that our economic problems are primarily the result of governmental intervention in the free market. For example, economist Walter Williams, in *The State Against Blacks*,[88] argues that minimum wage laws, occupational and business licensing of the taxicab industry, plumbers, and electricians, union policy in the railroad industry, truck regulation by the Interstate Commerce Commission, and other governmental regulations of the marketplace destroy opportunities for blacks to work. Economist Bruce L. Gardner has painstakingly analyzed agricultural policy in his book, *The Governing of Agriculture*, and concluded that "the search for solutions to agriculture's problems through government intervention has been and will continue to be a costly delusion."[89] And economist Charles Murray's remarkable and highly controversial book, *Losing Ground*,[90] shows most persuasively how the amalgam of social policy reforms from 1965 to 1970 actually made matters worse for the poor and minorities.[91] These are but a few examples and are not cited as the last word on these problems. They are only provided to indicate that many of the economic problems which the Catholic Bishops regard as morally intolerable are not necessarily the result of the workings of the free market. The status quo is indeed morally indefensible, but this does not mean that the free market is to blame.

Does the free market automatically produce justice? If we mean by this question to ask whether or not it is just, right for, or due human beings that they be able to conduct themselves freely, producing and exchanging goods and services according to their own judgments, then the answer is "yes." For the free market is nothing more than individual rights applied to the activities of producing and exchanging goods and services. If we mean to ask whether or not the people who produce and exchange goods and services in a free market automatically conduct themselves in a just manner, then the answer is "no." Whether dealing with goods and services in the marketplace or spouse and children in the family, people never automatically do what is just. The free market specifically, and individual rights generally, treat virtue (and vice) as something that only individual moral agents engage in.[92] The choices that individual human beings make in the market can be morally examined in order to see if they are just or unjust. The moral principles that underlie the free market—individual rights— can be evaluated and determined to be just or not. But the free market is neither just nor unjust, and there is no such thing as evaluating the morality of the free market *per se*. Unless one means to refer to the actions of moral agents in the marketplace or the moral principles which underlie the legal system that protects the free market, to talk of the justice or injustice of the free market is nonsense; for it hypostatizes the abstraction "free market." Neither markets nor collectivities are moral agents.

It is, however, the idea that virtue is not a collective phenomenon at all that makes the free market and the doctrine of individual rights so controversial; for it does not allow the state any role beyond the protection of individual rights in the promotion of virtue. Rather, the only things that remain to encourage virtue are persuasion and the free market. The Catholic Bishops clearly believe that this is not enough. They believe that the free market does not sufficiently promote justice, in part because of their theory of positive rights and in part because of how they interpret the functioning of the free market. Since the Catholic Bishops' theory of positive rights has already been examined, the following remarks shall be confined to an evaluation of their understanding of the free market.

First, it should be realized that even though economic transactions do not exhaust the ways people may relate to each other, there is really no such thing as an "economic side" to life that is separate from the other ends of life. Apart from the pathological case of the miser, "there is no 'economic motive' but only economic factors conditioning our striving to other ends. What in ordinary language is misleadingly called the 'economic motive' means merely the desire for general opportunity, the power to achieve unspecified ends."[93] There is no such thing as controlling the "economic side" of a person's life that would not involve controlling the entire life of a person. The Catholic Bishops cannot justifiably claim that government should only regulate the "economic side" of a person's life.

Second, there is a difference between economic power and political power. A free market measures economic power in terms of a person's ability to produce and exchange goods and services for which others will decide to trade. In a society that passes beyond barter and thus develops a higher standard of living through the division of labor, economic power is measured in terms of money. Money is a medium of exchange which facilitates trade, and when a market is not legally closed to competition and the money supply is not inflated by the government, having earned money indicates that one has succeeded in offering goods and services other people want.[94] The money, i.e., the economic power, one has in the free market is the result of the voluntary consent of those who are willing to trade their work or products—represented by money—for the work or products one is offering to sell. On the other hand, political power (or authority) is ultimately differentiated from other forms of power (or authority) by the fact that it uses physical force, compulsion, or coercion. When it is limited by a constitution that protects individual rights, political power is appropriate and necessary, but it is fundamentally different in kind from economic power. Though the Catholic Bishops acknowledge the great amount of wealth that people in the free market have produced, they neither acknowledge nor discuss the moral difference between economic power and political power.

Third, the wealth that people produce in the free market is not the result of people merely grabbing a larger share of earthly goods as, for example, a child might take a larger piece of pie than others. Natural resources are not human goods and do not satisfy human needs. They must be transformed into human goods by a process of thought and labor which individual human beings must perform. Human beings *create* wealth; they do not find it in nature like manna from heaven. If having vast amounts of natural resources were all that it took to fulfill human needs, then there would not be starving people in Africa. When the Catholic Bishops quote the Second Vatican Council's statement that everyone has a "right to have a share of earthly goods,"[95] they evade the entire question of what is necessary to *make use* of natural resources. A minimum of material goods is indeed an absolute necessity for human life, and this is why being able to freely create and exchange goods and services—that is to say, to participate in the free market—is so important.[96]

Fourth, the free market is not paternalistic and is thus an easy target for ethical criticism and, indeed, there are activities people engage in that should be criticized. Yet, what is crucial is to realize that the free market makes the moral evaluation of individual human behavior possible. If there were no free market, if there were instead only economic "planners" who directed what would be produced and exchanged, and if people were compelled to follow such directives, we would not morally evaluate the people who followed the directives. Rather, we would concentrate on the "planners." It would make no sense to criticize someone for failing to save for tomorrow (or for never spending money and hoarding it), or for failing to develop his talents (or for being so engrossed with the development of his abilities that he failed to develop friendships), or for failing to educate himself (or for becoming an "egghead" unable to relate to anything outside of his discipline), if his income, career, and educational level were determined by these economic "planners." The very ability to evaluate ethically the choices people exercise in the free market is testimony to its profound value. Personal moral advice that people give to one another on how they should live their lives would be senseless without a free market or, at least, would be confined to those areas of life, if there are any, untouched by economic factors. There would be no point to the Catholic Bishops telling people that they should share some of their income with those who are unfortunate if people did not have responsibility for earning and disposing of their wealth.[97]

Yet, it might be this very point that makes the Catholic Bishops call for government intervention in the lives and property of people. For to the extent that people have legal control over their property, others must deal with them by means of persuasion (and not coercion) when it comes to determining how that property will be used. The power of persuasion is, however, not something that is unimportant. As social and political animals, we are concerned with the actions of others. A person's actions are constantly being evaluated by others. In a society that protects individuals' rights, there would seem to be a greater concern for persuasive techniques than in a society which allows coercion. Indeed, in a free market persuasion is often used to accomplish numerous changes in people's behavior. The successful existence of charitable institutions is in fact a result of a free market—a result of the greater wealth created by people in the free market and of persuasive techniques used in asking people to help the unfortunate. Certainly, the Catholic Bishops should not underestimate the power of persuasion.

Fifth, the free market is often seen as a mere mechanism for satisfying people's desires and goals. If people have base desires, or if their goals never involve concern for others, then the free market will satisfy these desires and fulfill these goals without regard to their moral status. Accordingly, the free market is seen as encouraging all sorts of vices, e.g., lust, greed, selfishness, and materialism, and as not encouraging any social values. Yet, if the free market is examined more deeply and not treated as a mere mechanism, this view will be seen to be incorrect. There seems initially to be a confusion between what is permitted and what is encouraged. Though the free market permits many vices, it does not follow from this that it encourages vices. If a person must bear the consequences of her vices and cannot pass them on to others, e.g., the taxpayer, we certainly cannot say that such vices are encouraged by the free market.[98] Further, the fact that someone is ultimately responsible for the consequences of her actions in the free market is not without influence on the development of virtues. The free market is demanding. It requires that a person take responsibility for her life—viz., she determine her career, produce whatever is her unique talent to produce, and thus fashion a fulfilling life. The virtues of prudence, honesty, independence, thrift, and diligence, not to mention values of order and cooperation, are encouraged by the demands of the free market. The Catholic Bishops acknowledge the value of hard work and the importance of the wealth created by people in a free market, but they do not seem to recognize that the free market does encourage important moral virtues.

Sixth, it is important to realize that the free market constitutes only one way in which persons can relate to others. The primary concern in the marketplace is production and exchange. The nature of the relationship is neither one of animosity nor one of love. It is one of trade—the relationship is based on the mutual judgment that it is to the advantage of each. Trade is a morally legitimate way of relating to other human beings. It is a form of cooperation that can exist between people of vastly differing moral stances and world views. It is voluntary and respects the judgments of others, and does not preclude other ways of relating, e.g., love and concern. Though economic factors affect everything we do, economic production and exchange do not constitute all of life. Charity, generosity, concern, and benevolence are important virtues, and there is nothing about the free market that discourages their development. The Catholic Bishops are most correct in encouraging people to develop these virtues; nor does it seem that people in a free market are reluctant to develop them.

Seventh, there are no guarantees in life or in the free market. Thus, there may indeed be people in the free market who are in a helpless situation through no fault of their own. This is, however, true for any economic system. Further, simply because there are persons in a helpless situation, it does not necessarily follow that someone else is responsible for their plight. There is an important difference between circumstances that force people to be in need and people who use physical force or its threats to obtain values from others. The "coercion" of events should not be confused with the coercion of people.

The fact that businesses fail or industries change in a free market is nothing more than the result of people making new decisions on how they want to allocate their incomes for goods and services. Unless we assume that people have a right to a job, there is no reason to hold others responsible for the fact that someone is no longer able to keep a particular job because the firm he worked for could not stay in business. The nonperformance of certain activities—e.g., no longer buying a certain type of agricultural product—on the part of others does not violate this person's rights and is not something for which they are morally blameworthy. Furthermore, others should allocate their incomes in a way that best fills their needs and are under no obligation to continue to purchase the goods and services someone plays a role in producing. The person who loses his job should not give up and should look for work elsewhere. He should not expect that he has a right to have others take care of him. Others may, of course, choose to help a person who loses his job, and if the person is truly in need, they ought to help. Yet, there is nothing unjust about this situation. What is, of course, very unjust is the intervention of government into the free market, e.g., an embargo on trade with a foreign country, which can prevent people from earning a living and thus cause great suffering.

Government interference in the economic activities of human beings is, of course, the very thing that a free market would preclude, and it is the economic system that the Catholic Bishops should support if they are truly concerned with helping the poor. Yet, because the Catholic Bishops have accepted a doctrine of positive human rights, they consider the free market harsh. So, once again it is the issue of negative versus positive rights, and this dispute in turn revolves around what we take human dignity to be and to require. There is the crucial difference.

XI. Conclusion

The Catholic Bishops' *Economic Pastoral* successfully calls attention to the many needs of human beings. It also claims that human beings have many duties to themselves and others. These two points have been granted from the start. The Catholic Bishops have, however, failed to show that people have "economic rights," or positive rights. There may, for example, be duties to help those in need, but that does not by itself show that those in need have a right to assistance. The Catholic Bishops never successfully negotiated the transition from the adjectival sense of 'right' to the substantive sense of 'right.' They also failed to consider what these so-called "economic rights" would mean to the human dignity of those who would have to be used against their will. Further, the Catholic Bishops did not present a conception of the common good that could be regarded as truly common and, thus, good for each and every member of the political community. They did not, therefore, succeed in justifying their theory of rights in terms of the common good. Finally, the Catholic Bishops failed to sufficiently appreciate the virtues of the free market, or even to consider how it works, and thus ignored what may be the best way to deal with the problems that concern them.

Throughout this essay, an alternative moral vision has been sketched. It is incomplete and requires more support. Yet, the view of individual rights or negative rights that was presented does constitute an alternative to the view of rights that the Catholic Bishops have presented. Having an alternative view of rights is very important; for the Catholic Bishops are arguing for their policy proposals on moral grounds. Thus, they cannot be opposed merely on pragmatic grounds. It is with their moral vision that issue must be taken. This essay has done just that.[99]

PART 3

Response to Rasmussen

James Sterba

I think that both Douglas Rasmussen and I can agree that the U.S. Catholic bishops, in their *Economic Pastoral*, do not provide an adequate philosophical defense for their policy recommendations.[1] Where Rasmussen and I disagree is on the issue of whether an adequate philosophical defense for the policy recommendations of the *Economic Pastoral* can be provided. While Rasmussen denies that any such defense is available, I claim to have provided such a defense in my contribution to this volume.

In that contribution, I argue that an adequate defense of the policy recommendations of the *Economic Pastoral* can be provided by showing that a libertarian conception of human dignity, a welfare liberal conception of human dignity, and a socialist conception of human dignity, when they are correctly interpreted, all support the rights to welfare and affirmative action which are at the heart of the policy recommendations of the *Economic Pastoral*. In offering that defense, I argue, in particular, that a libertarian conception of human dignity supports both a right to welfare and a right to affirmative action through the application of the "ought implies can" principle to conflicts between the rich and the poor. On one interpretation, the principle supports these rights by favoring the liberty of the poor over the liberty of the rich. On another interpretation, it supports these rights by favoring a conditional right to property over an unconditional right to property. On either interpretation, what is crucial in the derivation of these rights is the claim that it would be unreasonable to ask the poor to accept anything less than these rights as the condition for their willing cooperation.

In his contribution to this volume, Rasmussen argues that to defend the policy recommendations of the *Economic Pastoral*, a theory of positive rights is required. But such a theory, Rasmussen contends, presents the defender of the policy recommendations of the *Economic Pastoral* with a dilemma:

(1) Either the rights of such a theory are taken to be absolute or they are taken to be supported, all things considered, by a standard of the common good.

(2) But if these rights are taken to be absolute they would be in conflict with the "ought implies can" principle, because under certain circumstances of scarce resources it would be impossible not to violate at least some of these rights.

(3) And if these rights are taken to be supported by a standard of the common good, such a standard would not be substantive enough to adequately support these rights.

Caught on the horns of this dilemma, Rasmussen contends, the bishops fail to "understand the basic character of human morality."

By contrast, Rasmussen defends a theory of absolute negative rights, according to which there are absolute negative rights to life, liberty, and property. These rights require that people not murder, assault, kidnap, or steal from one another. It follows from Rasmussen's account that any positive rights that exist are derivative; they are special rights which flow from the exercise of people's absolute negative rights. For example, if a person has a right to income from a pension, it flows from the exercise of her right to act freely and to choose to contribute to a pension fund to obtain such an income.

In defending the *Economic Pastoral* against Rasmussen's critique, I propose to show that in order to support the policy recommendations of the letter, there is no need ultimately to appeal to a theory of positive rights at all. Rather, to support the policy recommendations of the *Economic Pastoral* against libertarian critics, I claim that it suffices to show that these policy recommendations can be derived from a libertarian conception of human dignity. So in defending the *Economic Pastoral* against Rasmussen's critique, I will simply be continuing one line of argument I developed in my contribution to this volume.

Now, in his contribution to this volume, Rasmussen seeks to ground a theory of negative rights in a quasi-Aristotelian ideal of human flourishing. To quote Rasmussen:

[J]ust as human flourishing is the ultimate end or value of all human choices so must it also be that individual human beings exercising their own choices (and not those of others) while engaging in concrete activities that constitute their lives among others is of ultimate value.

Rasmussen further contends that the negative rights so derived from this ideal of human flourishing are absolute. But the sense in which Rasmussen understands these rights to be absolute is rather peculiar. Absolute rights and principles are typically understood to be rights and principles that hold under all conceivable circumstances.[2] For example, those who endorse as an absolute requirement the principle that one should never do evil that good may come of it, usually understand the principle in just this sense.[3] But this is not the way Rasmussen understands absolute rights and principles. According to Rasmussen, principles and rights can be absolute even if there are circumstances in which they can be disregarded.

But what are the circumstances in which absolute rights can be disregarded? Rasmussen characterizes such circumstances as "emergencies" and defines emergencies as circumstances where it is "impossible for the well-being of every person to be pursued and at the same time not interfere with the negative rights of others." Rasmussen further adds that "it makes no sense to say that the negative rights of others ought to be respected, if the terms under which negative rights are justified, viz., the pursuit of well-being, require that negative rights be ignored."

But this appears to be an extremely strong condition on the applicability of negative rights. According to this condition, respect for negative rights must serve the well-being of all the relevant parties before such rights would be in force. Of course, this condition on the applicability of negative rights could be easily satisfied if the notion of a person's well-being were already understood to be morally loaded in the strongest possible sense. For example, if a person's well-being were defined in terms of respect for the negative rights of others, then clearly a person's well-being would always require respect for negative rights. Even if the connection between a person's well-being and respect for negative rights were not that close as, for example, would be the case if a person's well-being were understood to involve simply having a good moral character, the requirement that the negative rights of others be respected might still not be that difficult to derive.[4] Actually, it is in this way that a straightforwardly Aristotelian defense of negative rights would proceed. In such an account, respect for negative rights would simply follow from a notion of well-being or happiness that was morally loaded in a fairly strong sense.[5]

But this is not the way that Rasmussen and other libertarians appear to want to ground their account of negative rights.[6] Rather, they appear to want to ground their account either in a morally neutral notion of a person's well-being or, at least, in a notion of well-being that is morally loaded in only a fairly weak sense; according to this weak sense, it does not follow from the fact that certain actions are morally good for people to do or refrain from doing that other people would be justified in forcing them to do or refrain from doing those actions. Rather, all that anyone would be justified in enforcing is what can be clearly shown to serve a person's well-being specified in a morally neutral sense.

This helps explain the attraction that some libertarians, such as Eric Mack and Tibor Machan (whom Rasmussen cites approvingly), seem to feel for ethical egoism, because that view also justifies its requirements in terms of a morally neutral account of well-being.[7] However, the problem with basing a theory of rights on such an account of a person's well-being is that each person will have reason to respect the rights of such a theory only to the extent that her interests are served by respecting those negative rights. If her interests are served well, she will have strong reasons to respect those rights, and if her interests are served poorly, she will have little or no reason to respect those rights.

Libertarians tend to recognize this consequence for their theory of negative rights with respect to emergency situations in which all parties affected have good reason not to respect the negative rights of others.[8] Tibor Machan, for instance, discusses the following example, drawn from Mack:

> [C]onsider the case of two men adrift on the open sea with a plank which can only support one man. Let us assume that in this case it serves the wellbeing of each man to survive, even if this survival costs the other's life. In this case, there is only one possible series of actions for each man that is sufficient for achieving his wellbeing. These actions are necessary for each of the men. In such an emergency case, rights are significantly absent. Each man ought, given the individualist principle and the assumptions in the case, to seek his own survival at the expense of the other. But neither can be said to have a right to survival. For to ascribe this right to either party would be to ascribe to the other party the obligation to allow the first party's survival at the expense of his own life. But the second party cannot be obligated to allow this, since we know that, given the individualist principle, he ought not to allow it.[9]

Machan agrees with Mack that in such cases negative rights do not apply, but only Mack seems to have recognized that inequalities between the rich and the poor can create analogous situations where the poor lack sufficient reason in terms of their own well-being for respecting the negative rights of the rich.[10] In such cases as well, Mack allows that rights are significantly absent.

Unfortunately, the situation is far worse for this attempt to ground a theory of negative rights on a morally neutral account of a person's well-being. For in addition to the implications of examples of the sort just discussed, it is also the case that unless a person's well-being is *best* served by respect for a particular system of negative rights, she will have good reason not to respect that system, either in whole or in part.

Nor will it do simply to point out, as Rasmussen does, that self-directedness or autonomy is constitutive of a person's well-being, whereas food, clothing, shelter, and the like are only necessary conditions for a person's well-being. Indeed, both are required for a person's well-being, and the degree of self-directedness or autonomy that is allowed some people, particularly the rich with respect to their surplus possessions, will determine how the poor will do with respect to their own well-being.[11] So if a theory of negative rights is to be justified in terms of serving the well-being of all the relevant parties, the rights sanctioned by that theory must *best* serve the well-being of *all* those parties.

Needless to say, this is a very difficult condition to fulfill. In fact, it is not clear that any system of rights would best serve the well-being of all the relevant parties. One system would best serve the well-being of some, another system would best serve the well-being of others, but it just seems unlikely that any system of rights would best serve the well-being of *all* the relevant parties! And if this is the case, it has devastating consequences for the theory of negative rights Rasmussen wants to defend: The absolute rights of this theory would be, for the most part, inapplicable because the condition for their applicability—that respect for them best serves the well-being of all the relevant parties—would rarely, if ever, obtain. Certainly this would be a theory of absolute rights in name only, if there ever was one. Of course, Rasmussen does not recognize that these are the implications of the theory of rights he defends, but they follow from his account nonetheless.

By contrast, the negative rights that are in fact derivable from the libertarian conception of human dignity are absolute in the strongest possible sense: they apply under all conceivable circumstances. The principal rights of this sort are (1) the right of the deserving rich not to be interfered with unless the basic needs of the deserving poor have yet to be met, and (2) the right of the deserving poor not to be interfered with when they are fairly taking from the surplus possessions of those with more than enough resources in order to satisfy their basic needs.[12] The deserving rich are those who acquired their surplus possessions by morally legitimate means, and the deserving poor are those who have used all the morally legitimate means otherwise available to them for meeting their basic needs.

One reason why these rights, which I claim are derivable from a libertarian conception of human dignity, are absolute is that they are nuanced in ways that the rights Rasmussen defends are not. But the more important reason why these rights are absolute is that their justification does not, like the rights Rasmussen defends, depend upon their best serving everyone's well-being in a morally neutral sense. For example, recognizing the rights of the deserving rich not to be interfered with unless the basic needs of the deserving poor have yet to be met may well conflict with the interest of the deserving poor in obtaining an even greater share of wealth. Similarly, recognizing the rights of the deserving poor not to be interfered with when they fairly take from the surplus possessions of those with more than enough resources in order to satisfy their basic needs may well conflict with the interest of the deserving rich in retaining and enjoying their surplus possessions. But recognizing these rights will be justified nonetheless, because their justification does not depend upon their best serving the well-being of everyone but, rather, upon what is required by the "ought implies can" principle. Since it would be unreasonable to ask the deserving poor to forgo the right not to be interfered with when they fairly take from the surplus possessions of those with more than enough resources in order to satisfy their basic needs, and it would *not* be unreasonable to ask the deserving rich to forgo any conflicting interest, this right is required by the libertarian conception of human dignity. Likewise, since it would be unreasonable to ask the deserving rich to forgo the right not to be interfered with unless the basic needs of the deserving poor have yet to be met, and it would *not* be unreasonable to ask the deserving poor to forgo any conflicting interests, this right is also required by the libertarian conception of human dignity. So the contrast could not be greater between the absolute rights which emerge from a libertarian conception of human dignity as I understand it and the seemingly absolute-in-name-only rights which emerge from Rasmussen's account.

It might be objected that even if I am right that absolute negative welfare rights would emerge from a libertarian conception of human dignity, these rights would still fall short of the positive welfare rights that Rasmussen claims are needed to support the policy recommendations of the *Economic Pastoral*. The difference is that a person's negative welfare right can be violated only when other people interfere through acts of commission with the person's exercise of that right, whereas a person's positive welfare right can be violated not only by acts of commission, but by acts of omission as well. However, as I argued before, this difference will have little practical import. For once libertarians come to recognize the legitimacy of a negative welfare right, then in order not to be subject to the poor person's discretion in choosing when and how to exercise her negative welfare right, libertarians will tend to favor two morally legitimate ways of preventing the exercise of such rights. First, libertarians can provide the poor with mutually beneficial job opportunities. Second, libertarians can institute an adequate positive welfare right that would make it impossible to satisfy the fairness requirement of the poor person's negative welfare right. Accordingly, if libertarians adopt either or both of these ways of legitimately preventing the poor from exercising their negative welfare rights, libertarians will end up endorsing the same sort of welfare institutions favored by welfare liberals.

It might also be objected that the negative rights that I claim are derivable from a libertarian conception of human dignity are not absolute when they are applied to the type of emergency situations that concern libertarians like Mack, Machan, and Rasmussen. (What, for instance, do these rights require in Mack's example of two persons adrift at sea with a plank which can only support one of them?) But since it is presumably the basic needs of both parties that are involved, the two rights of my account that I have so far specified do not apply in such a case. Notice, however, that it is not that we think that such rights should apply, and it turns out that they do not, as in the case of the rights Mack, Machan, and Rasmussen defend. Rather, these rights apply specifically to situations in which resources are available to meet the basic needs of all parties if they are distributed correctly; they are not directly applicable to situations of radical scarcity.

Further, even in such cases of radical scarcity, a libertarian conception of human dignity would provide a solution, and it would be different from the one proposed by Mack and seconded by Machan and Rasmussen. In Mack's solution, since the well-being of each party is fundamentally in conflict, each person is permitted, even obligated, to do whatever she can to preserve her own well-being, even if that involves killing the other person. In contrast, the libertarian conception of human dignity I am defending would severely limit what one party could do to the other, even in pursuit of her fundamental well-being. Accordingly, applying this conception to Mack's case, a struggle for the plank would be in order, yet one party could not kill the other to secure the plank. Similarly, if in an emergency situation people have already legitimately acquired resources that are just sufficient to meet, say, their basic nutritional needs and can produce no more, other people, on my account, have no right to take away those resources. On Mack, Machan, and Rasmussen's account, such actions *would* be morally permissible.

Finally, it might be objected to my libertarian defense of the policy recommendations of the *Economic Pastoral* that although the negative rights I have articulated do emerge from the application of the "ought implies can" principle as I have interpreted it, my interpretation of the principle is itself question-begging. Thus, it might be argued that while the principle can plausibly be interpreted to exclude from the scope of enforceable moral obligations actions that are logically, physically, or psychologically impossible, it is question-begging to interpret the principle as also excluding actions that are merely unreasonable or unreasonable to ask of people.

But why would this be a question-begging interpretation to use against a libertarian opponent? One might contend that for libertarians, putting forth a moral ideal means no more than being willing to universalize one's fundamental commitments. Surely we have no difficulty imagining the rich willing to universalize their commitments to relatively strong property rights. Yet, at the same time, we have no difficulty imagining the poor and their advocates willing to universalize their commitments to relatively weak property rights. Consequently, if the libertarian's moral ideal is interpreted in this fashion, it would not be able to provide a basis for reasonably resolving conflicts of interest between the rich and the poor. But without such a basis for conflict resolution, how could societies flourish, as libertarians claim they would, under a minimal state, or no state at all?[13] Surely, in order for societies to flourish in this fashion, the libertarian ideal must resolve conflicts of interest in ways that it would be reasonable to ask everyone affected to accept. But, as we have seen, that requirement can only be satisfied if the rich sacrifice the liberty to meet some of their luxury needs so the poor can have the liberty to meet their basic needs.

In conclusion, I have argued that Rasmussen's critique of the U.S. Catholic Bishops' *Economic Pastoral* can be defeated by the philosophical counterpart to an end run. Thus, while not contesting that the bishops have failed to provide an adequate philosophical defense of the policy recommendations of their *Economic Pastoral*, I have contended that an adequate philosophical defense can be provided by appealing to a libertarian conception of human dignity, a socialist conception of human dignity, and a welfare liberal conception of human dignity. In particular, to meet the libertarian challenge to the *Economic Pastoral*, I have argued that a libertarian conception of human dignity, containing absolute negative rights, supports a right to welfare and a right to affirmative action, which are central to the policy recommendations of the *Economic Pastoral*. I have challenged Rasmussen's own theory of absolute negative rights which, he claims, rejects the policy recommendations of the *Economic Pastoral* on two points. First, I argued that this theory of negative rights is not adequately grounded in an account of a person's well-being, as Rasmussen claims. Second, I argued that the rights of this theory appear to be absolute in name only. I claim that these two interconnected problems with Rasmussen's own theory of negative rights, joined with my libertarian defense of the policy recommendations of the *Economic Pastoral*, suffice to undermine Rasmussen's critique.

PART 4

Response to Sterba

Douglas Rasmussen

James Sterba notes that the conclusions of the Catholic Bishops' Pastoral, *Economic Justice for All: Catholic Social Teaching and the U.S. Economy*, are not adequately justified from a philosophical point of view. Since the Catholic Bishops seek the cooperation and support of those who do not share their faith and tradition and since the Catholic Bishops claim that their views can be supported by philosophical argumentation, it is important that something be done. Sterba proposes to provide the missing philosophical defense. In this response, I propose to examine Sterba's defense.

Sterba proposes to defend the conclusions of the *Economic Pastoral* by showing that each of three different and apparently competing conceptions of human dignity, when they are properly interpreted, support the conclusion that persons have "economic rights." Sterba identifies three basic conceptions of human dignity: a libertarian conception of human dignity, a socialist conception of human dignity, and a welfare liberal conception of human dignity. He distinguishes each conception of human dignity by the political ideal it advances. The political ideals advanced by these three basic conceptions of human dignity are respectively: liberty, equality, and a blend of liberty and equality which is characterized as "contractual fairness." Sterba claims that all assignments of rights and duties are ultimately to be justified in terms of these political ideals.

After describing what the political ideals of each of these apparently competing conceptions of human dignity imply for public policy, Sterba seeks to show not the superiority of any one of these conceptions but, rather, how these conceptions can be reconciled on the practical level. As Sterba states the point:

> [I]t does not matter whether one endorses liberty, equality, or contractual
> fairness as the ultimate political ideal, because all three of these ideals,
> when correctly interpreted, support the same practical requirements, and
> turn out to be the standardly acknowledged practical requirements of a
> welfare liberal conception of human dignity, namely, a right to welfare and
> a right to affirmative action.

Sterba examines both the libertarian and socialist conceptions of human
dignity in order to show that these conceptions do indeed support the
practical requirements of the welfare liberal conception of human dignity.

Sterba begins with an examination of the ideal of liberty of a libertarian
conception of human dignity. He distinguishes between two approaches in
taking liberty as the ultimate political ideal: (1) the view which takes the
right to liberty as basic and defines all other rights in terms of this right;
and (2) the view which takes the right to life and property as basic and
defines all other rights, including the right to liberty, in terms of this set of
rights. In what follows, I will consider Sterba's analysis of each of these
approaches to liberty. I will not consider his examination of the ideal of
equality of the socialist conception of human dignity.

Sterba argues that in a situation in which Smith has more resources than
he needs to meet his basic nutritional needs and Jones does not have
sufficient resources to meet his basic nutritional needs, there is a conflict of
liberties. He holds that the libertarian uncritically assumes that liberty
always has priority over other political and social ideals and that the liberty
of the poor is not at stake in such situations. Yet, Sterba insists that "what is
at stake is the liberty of the poor to take from the surplus possessions of the
rich what is necessary to satisfy their basic nutritional needs." Given that
there is such a conflict of liberties, which liberty is morally preferable: the
liberty of the rich to use their resources as they see fit or the liberty of the
poor to take resources from the rich sufficient to meet their basic needs?
Sterba holds that the liberty of the poor to take from the surplus resources
of others what is required to meet their basic nutritional needs is morally
preferable.

He attempts to show that the liberty of the poor to take surplus resources
from the rich to meet their basic needs is the morally preferable liberty by
an appeal to the "ought implies can" principle. He interprets this principle
to mean that "people are not morally required to do what they lack the
power to do or what would involve so great a sacrifice that it would be
unreasonable to ask them to perform such an action." Sterba claims that it
is unreasonable to ask the poor to willingly relinquish their liberty to take
from the rich what they need to meet their basic nutritional needs and, by
contrast, that it is not unreasonable to ask the rich to sacrifice the liberty to

protect their surplus resources so that the poor may have their basic nutritional needs met. If we assume that a moral ideal cannot violate the "ought implies can" principle and remain a moral ideal, then the ideal of liberty must favor, as Sterba argues, "the liberty of the poor over the liberty of the rich."

If it is unreasonable to ask the poor to forgo their liberty to take from the rich, then the libertarian ideal of liberty cannot resolve the conflict. A moral ideal resolves conflicts of interest in ways that it would be reasonable for everyone affected to accept. Yet, as long as libertarians attempt to put forward a moral ideal, "they cannot," Sterba states, "allow that it would be unreasonable *both* to ask the rich to sacrifice the liberty to meet some of their luxury needs in order to benefit the poor and to ask the poor to sacrifice the liberty to meet their basic needs in order to benefit the rich." Sterba concludes that by any neutral assessment, it must be the rich who are asked to sacrifice their liberty and not the poor and, thus, that the libertarian ideal of liberty requires the recognition of economic rights.

Sterba also claims that the libertarian ideal of liberty requires the recognition of economic rights even if liberty is defined in terms of rights. If the right to life is the right not to be killed unjustly, and the right to property is the right to acquire goods and resources either by initial acquisitions or voluntary transactions, and if these rights are not understood as being violated when defensive measures are used to protect a person from life-threatening attacks or his property from theft, there is nonetheless still a conflict. When Smith attempts to protect his surplus resources from Jones's efforts to take them, there is a conflict of rights. When the rich prevent the poor from taking what they require to satisfy their basic nutritional needs, the rich are resisting life-preserving activities of the poor and, according to Sterba: "when the poor do die as a consequence of such acts, it seems clear that the rich would be killing the poor, whether intentionally or unintentionally." Whose right is morally preferable: the right of the rich to protect their property and thus kill the poor, or the right of the poor to secure the resources they need to fulfill their basic nutritional needs and thus prevent the rich from enjoying luxury goods?

Sterba again appeals to the "ought implies can" principle in order to resolve this conflict. This time he uses this principle to assess two opposing accounts of property rights: (1) an account which holds that the right to property is *not* conditional upon whether other persons have sufficient opportunities and resources to satisfy their basic needs; and (2) an account which holds that initial acquisition and voluntary transactions confer title on all resources except those surplus resources which, as Sterba puts it, "are required to satisfy the basic needs of those poor who, through no fault of their own, lack the opportunities and resources to satisfy their own basic needs." Sterba claims that to accept the first account of property rights would be to justify killing the poor (as a consequence of the rich protecting their property) and, thus, that it would be unreasonable to ask the poor to accept some version of property rights other than the second. Sterba also notes that it does not matter whether the rich kill the poor or only mentally and physically debilitate them. If the poor are prevented from taking the needed surplus resources of the rich, they are rendered incapable of acquiring property and, thus, property rights are precluded from arising for them. According to Sterba, the first account of property clearly imposes an unreasonable sacrifice upon the poor. If liberty is to be a moral ideal, and if liberty is understood in terms of the right to life and to property, the second account of property rights—the one favored by the poor—must be accepted. Despite what libertarians claim, Sterba believes that their political ideal of liberty requires the recognition of economic rights.

Sterba's analysis of the so-called libertarian conception of human dignity and his claim that the political ideal of liberty requires recognition of economic rights is no doubt accurate and true for *some* conception of libertarianism. Yet, his analysis and claim is neither accurate nor true for all conceptions of libertarianism.

Libertarian, like *liberal*, is no univocal notion. If we are to understand what is actually meant by calling a theory *libertarian* or *liberal*, it is necessary to examine the normative theory and conception of human dignity used by the theorist whose position is so called. Only in this way can one understand what the theorist means by the word *liberty*, the word which is presumably the basis for his position being characterized as libertarian or liberal.

If liberty is understood as simply the state of being unconstrained by other persons from doing what one wants, there is an immediate problem: whose liberty is morally preferable? Is Smith's liberty to prevent Jones from taking his resources or Jones's liberty to take Smith's resources to be morally preferred? Smith wants to keep his resources, and Jones wants to take them. When liberty is understood, without any normative understanding of the terms employed in the definition, as simply the state of being unconstrained by other persons from exercising the power to do whatever one wants, all wants and actions are normatively equal. There is no way the ideal of liberty can determine which want or action is morally preferable.

Yet, the problem is not just normative; it is conceptual as well. Disagreements about when liberty has been restrained cannot be arbitrated, nor can we even reach agreement on the description of a situation as a conflict of liberties, if there is no basis for determining and legitimizing the valuation that is placed on various activities people undertake. For example, is liberty being restrained or heightened when the government, through increased taxation and transfer payments, provides the needy with food, clothing, housing, and education? The Libertarian Party libertarian says not, while the Sterba libertarian says that it is. The classical liberal says not, while the contemporary American liberal says that it is. Appealing to what is "conducive to liberty" will not help; for in this situation, we are trying to determine what liberty is.[1] Deeper issues, such as the nature of human dignity and its normative basis, need to be considered if liberty is to be a moral and political ideal, and if *libertarian* or *liberal* are to be more than equivocal notions.

Despite appearances, Sterba never states what the so-called libertarian conception of human dignity is. In fact, the only way the various conceptions of human dignity are differentiated is in terms of the political ideal they promote. There is no deeper consideration of what it is about human dignity that makes liberty a political ideal. Nor is there any discussion of what it is about human beings and their flourishing that give rise to human dignity. We are to take liberty as an ideal without any discussion of what normative or metaphysical basis there might be for considering it an ideal.

Sterba's commitment to Rawlsian contractarianism is most likely the reason for this lack of deeper normative and metaphysical speculation. Yet it should be noted that Sterba's failure to consider some of the deeper issues underlying the ideal of liberty that are discussed in my essay in this volume causes his analysis of the so-called libertarian conception of human dignity to bear little resemblance to the libertarian position developed in my essay. Sterba's claim that a commitment to the ideal of liberty requires recognizing economic rights is not true of the view of liberty presented in my essay nor of the views of liberty presented in the writings of many other libertarian theorists.[2] This critique will, however, be confined to showing why Sterba's analysis and claim do not apply to the position presented and defended in my essay.

In what follows, the first five remarks will differentiate the libertarian position defended in my essay from Sterba's account of the libertarian conception of human dignity; the remaining remarks will show why the position defended in my essay does not need to recognize economic rights.

1. The rights to life, liberty, and property are the moral and political ideals presented and defended in my essay. There was no attempt to define "liberty" in terms of these rights; rather, these rights were defended as moral and political ideals in and of themselves. Thus, there is a sense in which the position taken in my essay could be called "libertarian" and a

sense in which it could not. The position developed and defended in my essay is "libertarian" if and only if "libertarian" is taken as the position which upholds these rights as the ultimate political ideal. The position is not "libertarian" if there is supposed to be some non-normative understanding of "liberty" to which one is committed and for which one is trying to find some normative justification.

2. These rights to life, liberty, and property are basic, universal, and negative. They are rights to actions: the right to take all the actions necessary for the support and furtherance of one's life; and the right to the action of producing or earning something and keeping, using, and disposing of it according to one's goals. To have these rights morally sanctions the freedom to act on one's voluntary, uncoerced choice for one's own goals. To have a right in this sense morally obligates others to abstain from physical compulsion, coercion, or interference or the threat thereof. Such action may only be taken in defense of these rights and only against those who have violated rights. These rights are, therefore, *claim-rights* and are thus differentiated from a Hobbesian conception of rights by the fact that they are necessarily linked with the duty of other people to refrain from using people for purposes they have not chosen.

The fact that these rights are claim-rights does not, however, imply that they can be translated without remainder into duty claims; for these rights are not justified on the basis of what one person owes another but, rather, on a person's principled pursuit of his own fulfillment. Thus, I argued in my essay that the very proposition that a person must invoke to morally justify pursuit of his own flourishing shows that one would be unjustified in using others for purposes they have not chosen. To do so would violate *their* rights to life, liberty, and property.

3. In his analysis of the view which takes the right to liberty as basic, Sterba states that "libertarians assume that the liberty of the poor is not at stake in such conflict situations." The type of conflict situation that Sterba has in mind, and one that will be used repeatedly in discussing Sterba's views, is one in which Smith has more resources than what he needs to meet his basic nutritional needs but wants to keep these resources for his own uses, and Jones does not have sufficient resources to meet his basic nutritional needs and wants to take Smith's surplus resources.[3] Jones acts to take Smith's resources and Smith acts to stop Jones. But when Sterba analyzes such conflict situations, he makes no mention of the *right* to liberty, but only of liberties; if the situation that exists between Smith and Jones is examined in terms of the *right* to liberty, there is no conflict of rights between Smith and Jones, but only a conflict of wants and actions, viz., non-normative liberties. As I already indicated, the right to liberty is a

claim-right and is not simply the right to do anything one pleases. Sterba views the situation between Smith and Jones either as a conflict of non-normative liberties or as a conflict of liberties normatively understood. If the former, then his analysis is irrelevant to the libertarian position presented in my essay. If the latter, then his description of the situation as a "conflict" is, to say the least, problematic.

There may be some question as to whether Smith may not in the past have violated Jones's right to liberty and thereby caused his difficulties, but in the situation described it is a violation of Smith's right to liberty if Jones acts to take some of his property. Yet, if this account of the situation is to be fully appreciated, the rights to life and property need to be examined. I will undertake this shortly.

4. The normative basis for the rights to life, liberty, and property is linked to the notion of "justice" *if* justice is understood as the act of giving others their due and *if* the notion of "due" is understood as being determined by the nature of human fulfillment or flourishing. This does not, however, imply that rights are assigned by appealing to what justice requires in each situation, or even by what rational contractors behind a veil of ignorance would view as just. Instead, these rights are understood as setting forth the moral space that all human beings have due them if the highly individualized and self-directed character of their natural function—human flourishing—is to have any possibility of being achieved when they live among others who can exercise control over what they do and when such community life is possible. In other words, a person has these rights not because they will be invariably used in a just way, but because they constitute the social and political expression of the claim that there is no higher moral purpose, no other end to be served than the individual human being's self-initiated and self-maintained achievement of his individuative and generic potentialities. Rights are thus understood as the political conditions which must exist if people are to have any chance to be just; they are not merely entitlements assigned them on the basis of what justice requires.

5. The normative standard used in developing and defending the rights to life, liberty, and property was human fulfillment or flourishing. This standard is not the same as having one's basic nutritional needs met, viz., physical survival, or even having what it takes to live well. When assessing whether one's duty to fulfill the obligations these rights require involves so great a sacrifice that it is unreasonable, it is vital to be clear regarding the normative standard that is to be used in making this assessment. If we are to evaluate the rights to life, liberty, and property in terms of the normative foundation used to develop and defend them, the determination that a

duty required by these rights involves so great a sacrifice that it is unreasonable to require it should be based on the account of human flourishing that was used, not some other standard. This is not to say that someone cannot advance another normative standard to make this judgment. But it is to say that when this is done, we should not be too surprised if the duties required by these rights no longer seem reasonable.

6. When assessing whether it is reasonable to require Jones, who does not have sufficient resources to meet his basic nutritional needs, to abstain from taking Smith's resources, which are more than what he needs to meet his basic nutritional needs, Sterba uses the standard of physical survival to determine whether this duty is reasonable. There is no reason why Sterba cannot advance physical survival as the normative standard by which to judge whether certain moral duties are reasonable. Yet, if Sterba's argument against the reasonableness of the duties the rights to life, liberty, and property require is to have weight, Sterba needs to show (1) why this standard is to be accepted and (2) why it is preferable to other normative standards, especially human flourishing. Sterba never addresses these issues in his essay.

7. If human beings are to have any chance of flourishing, the right to live one's life according to one's own choices must be respected; and since human beings are not disembodied ghosts, but flesh and blood creatures whose autonomy or self-directedness pertains to psychic states *and* to actions that occur at some place and some time and which employ or involve material things, the right to life entails the right to use one's time and resources according to one's own judgment. The right to property is not the right to an object, or even to the use of an object, but to the action and the consequence of producing or earning that object.[4] It is, therefore, not objects *per se* that an individual needs to have rights to, as if any random distribution were acceptable. A human being needs to maintain control of what he has earned or produced through his self-directed or autonomous action in the material world. Human flourishing is not merely intellectual contemplation.

If the foregoing paragraph is essentially correct, respect for the right to property is absolutely crucial if human flourishing is to exist. It is, therefore, not unreasonable to hold that the right to property is not conditional on other human beings having sufficient opportunities and resources to satisfy their basic needs. People ought not to be used by other people for purposes they have not chosen, and this most definitely means that a person's property is not to be used for purposes the person has not agreed to. A person's choices and judgments cannot be said to have been respected if the material expression of those judgments is itself divested from the individual.

Unless we are to assume that people have a positive right to opportunities and resources and then beg the question against the libertarian
position, or unless we are talking about an emergency situation,[5] which I
have described in my essay, it is unreasonable for Jones to decide not to
fulfill his obligation to respect the property rights of Smith. Assuming that
Jones's unfortunate condition is not the result of some previous violations
of his negative rights to life, liberty, and property (which is many times not
the case in the world today), the reasonable and morally correct thing to do for
Jones to do is to ask for help and assistance from others and to try to do
everything he can to earn what it takes to meet his needs. He should tell
others how, through a series of unfortunate circumstances, through no fault
of his own, he finds himself in this desperate situation. He should ask for
any work he can find and try to discover how he might be able to improve
his situation. Sterba's account is vague as to whether such possibilities exist
for Jones, and it is just on the basis of such details that the force of Sterba's
appeal to the "ought implies can" principle rests. If there are such possibilities, Sterba's argument that it would be reasonable for someone like
Jones to ignore the property rights of others fails.

If there are no such possibilities, if there is *no* way Jones might pursue his
natural end and respect Smith's rights, and if Jones is not responsible for
bringing about the desperate situation in which he finds himself, then
Smith cannot claim to have his rights violated if Jones should attempt to
take some of his resources. Yet, this does not show, as Sterba claims, that
Jones has a right to take Smith's "surplus" resources and thus that there is a
conflict between the rights of Smith (the rich) and Jones (the poor). Nor
does this show that Smith could not legitimately (on the basis of his own
human flourishing) defend his resources. Rather, it shows that not all situations can be approached in social and political terms—rights are absolute
but not applicable to every possible situation—and that Jones would after-
ward have the burden of showing a court of law that the situation was
indeed one which he was not responsible for bringing about and which in
no way afforded other possible courses of action. Further, it must be remembered that rights claims do not exhaust ethics, and Smith and Jones
should try, as best the circumstances will permit, to determine the morally
proper course of action. Yet, such decisions in such situations do not by
their very nature provide any basis for the determination of public *policy*
and thus do not support Sterba's claim that the libertarian conception of
human dignity, when properly interpreted, requires the recognition of
"economic rights."

8. When Smith prevents Jones from taking his resources and Jones, as a
consequence of being unable to obtain resources sufficient to meet his
basic nutritional needs, dies or becomes so debilitated that he cannot ac-

quire any property, Jones's rights to life, liberty, and property have not been violated by Smith. Jones has no positive right to life, liberty, or property. He has only negative rights. Sterba suggests, by the use of a rhetorical question, that Jones's rights would be violated by Smith in this situation. It is not at all clear what basis Sterba has for this suggestion. Since Sterba seeks to show how the libertarian conception of human dignity requires the recognition of positive economic rights, he cannot interpret the rights to life, liberty, and property as positive rights without begging the question. Further, since Sterba is no longer dealing with the conflicts that result from some non-normative notion of liberty, but with the rights to life, liberty, and property, he needs to show how Jones's rights have been violated by Smith's action.[6] He does not do this in his analysis of the view that the rights to life and property are basic. He merely suggests that Jones's rights have been violated by Smith's acts of self-defense and continues his argument as if this point has been established. Yet this is the very point that is at issue.

9. These remarks should not be construed to imply that the libertarian position developed and presented in my essay is not subject to serious challenge or does not face difficulties. Rather, these remarks have been aimed only at Sterba's claim that the libertarian conception of human dignity, when it is properly interpreted, supports the Catholic Bishops' claim that people have economic rights. These remarks have shown that there is a position which would generally be regarded as libertarian for which Sterba's claim is not true. Since Sterba did not seek to defend the claims of the Catholic Bishops by showing the superiority of the welfare liberal conception of human dignity over competing conceptions, his failure to show why a libertarian position such as the one presented in my essay must recognize economic rights only emphasizes the central claim of my essay—namely, that the moral vision of the United States Catholic Bishops is seriously flawed and is ultimately at odds with the dignity of the individual human being.

NOTES

Introduction

1. National Conference of Catholic Bishops, *Economic Justice for All: Catholic Social Teaching and the U.S. Economy* (Third Draft), *Origins*, vol. 16 (June 5, 1986) [hereinafter referred to as the *Economic Pastoral*]. Although there was subsequently a fourth and final draft published, it did not differ significantly from the third draft; all references in this volume are to the third draft.

2. *ibid.*, p. 36.

3. *ibid.*, pp. 36, 37.

4. *ibid.*, p. 37.

5. *ibid.*, p. 36.

6. *ibid.*, p. 41.

7. *ibid.*, p. 40.

8. *ibid.*

9. *ibid.*, p. 41.

10. *ibid.*

11. *ibid.*, p. 47.

12. *ibid.*

13. *ibid.*, p. 48.

14. *ibid.*

15. *ibid.*, p. 49.

16. *ibid.*, p. 51.

17. *ibid.*

18. *ibid.*, p. 56.

19. *ibid.*, p. 57.

104   NOTES

Part 1

1. National Conference of Catholic Bishops, *Economic Justice for All: Catholic Social Teaching and the U.S. Economy* (Third Draft), *Origins*, vol. 16 (June 5, 1986) [hereinafter referred to as the *Economic Pastoral*].

2. Rembert Weakland, "The Church and Economics" (lecture delivered at the University of Notre Dame, February 7, 1985), p. 6.

3. *Economic Pastoral*, p. 36.

4. *ibid.*

5. *ibid.*

6. *ibid.*, p. 40.

7. *ibid.*, p. 42.

8. Charles Krauthammer, "Perils of the Prophet Motive," *The New Republic*, vol. 182 (December 24, 1984), p. 12. Krauthammer raises other objections to the *Economic Pastoral*, but the one cited is his most distinctive objection.

9. Thomas Reese, "The Bishops on the Economy: What Next," *America*, vol. 153 (February 2, 1985), p. 78.

10. Mario M. Cuomo, "Toward a Consensus," *America*, vol. 153 (January 12, 1985), p. 11.

11. On this point, see Weakland, "The Church and Economics," pp. 8-9.

12. *Economic Pastoral*, p. 60.

13. Joseph A. Califano, Jr., "The Prophets and the Profiters," *America*, vol. 153 (January 12, 1985), p. 6.

14. Andrew Greeley, "The Bishops and the Economy: a 'Radical' Dissent," *America*, vol. 153 (January 12, 1985), pp. 19-20.

15. *Economic Pastoral*, p. 46. Similar statements can be found in earlier versions of the letter.

16. *ibid.*, p. 42.

17. Greeley, "The Bishops and the Economy," p. 21.

18. *Economic Pastoral*, p. 51.

19. Charles Murray, *Losing Ground* (New York: Basic Books, 1984), pp. 8-9.

20. Michael Harrington, "Crunched Numbers," *The New Republic*, vol. 193 (January 28, 1985), p. 8.

21. Christopher Jencks, "How Poor are the Poor?" *New York Review of Books*, vol. 32 (May 9, 1985), p. 44.

22. This view would be rejected by the authors of *Toward the Future: Catholic Social Thought and the U.S. Economy*, the Lay Commission on Catholic Social Teaching and the U.S. Economy, reprinted in *Catholicism in Crisis*, vol. 2 (November 1984). But at least some of the biblical basis for their somewhat different policy recommendations has been shown to rest on poor exegesis. See Dennis Hamm, "Economic Policy and the Uses of Scripture," *America*, vol. 153 (May 4, 1985), pp. 368-371.

23. Notice that all that I am claiming is that the welfare liberal's ideal *can be characterized* as contractual fairness, not that it must be so characterized. Nevertheless, welfare liberals like Bruce Ackerman and Ronald Dworkin who have attempted to characterize the welfare liberal ideal differently have, it turns out, not departed radically from a contractual fairness formulation. See,

Bruce Ackerman, *Social Justice and the Liberal State* (New Haven: Yale University Press, 1980) and Ronald Dworkin, "What is Equality? Part I & II," *Philosophy & Public Affairs*, vol. 10 (1981), pp. 185-246, 283-345.

24. In Chapters 9 and 10 of *How to Make People Just* (forthcoming), I argue that both communitarian and feminist conceptions of human dignity can be reconciled with a welfare liberal conception of human dignity.

25. John Hospers, *Libertarianism* (Los Angeles: Nash, 1971), pp. 5, 10, 50-51. There is a disagreement among libertarians concerning what is involved in taking liberty as the ultimate political ideal. One view, which I devote more time to here, takes a right to liberty as basic and defines all other rights in terms of that right. The other view takes a set of rights typically including a right to life and a right to property as basic and then defines all other rights, including a right to liberty, in terms of this set of rights. I discuss this latter view on pp. 33-34.

26. Isaiah Berlin, *Four Essays on Liberty* (Oxford: Oxford University Press, 1969), pp. xxxix-xl.

27. John Hospers, "What Libertarianism Is," Tibor Machan, ed., *The Libertarian Alternative* (Chicago: Nelson-Hall, 1974), p. 13; Robert Nozick, *Anarchy, State, and Utopia* (New York: Basic Books, 1974), p. 179n.

28. Milton Friedman, *Capitalism and Freedom* (Chicago: University of Chicago Press, 1962), pp. 161-172; Nozick, *Anarchy, State, and Utopia*, pp. 160-164.

29. Karl Marx, *Critique of the Gotha Program*, ed. C.P. Dutt (New York: International Publishers, 1966).

30. For a discussion of worker control, see Barry Clark and Herbert Gintis, "Rawlsian Justice and Economic Systems," *Philosophy & Public Affairs*, vol. 7 (1978), pp. 302-325; Harry Braveman, *Labor and Monopoly Capitalism* (New York: Monthly Review Press, 1974); Carole Pateman, *Participation and Democratic Theory* (New York: Cambridge University Press, 1970); *Work in America*, Report of the Special Task Force of the Secretary of Health, Education and Welfare (Cambridge: M.I.T., 1973).

31. Edward Nell and Onora O'Neill, "Justice Under Socialism," James P. Sterba, ed., *Justice: Alternative Political Perspectives* (Belmont: Wadsworth Publishing Co., 1980), pp. 200-210.

32. For reasons why a social program which guarantees a right to welfare and a right to affirmative action does not appear to go far enough, see John H. Schaar, "Equality of Opportunity and Beyond," Roland Pennock and John Chapman, eds., *Equality* (New York: Atherton Press, 1967).

33. C.B. Macpherson, *Democratic Theory* (Oxford: Oxford University Press, 1973).

34. C.B. Macpherson, *Property* (Toronto: University of Toronto Press, 1978).

35. Carol Gould, *Marx's Social Ontology* (Cambridge: M.I.T., 1978).

36. *ibid.*, p. 171.

37. Of course, there are other contemporary social contract theories, but these views are not offered as a proper blend of the libertarian's ideal of liberty and the socialist's ideal of equality. For example, in his most recent book, *Morality by Agreement* (Oxford: Oxford University Press, 1986), David Gauthier attempts to ground his social contract theory in rational self-interest, and James Buchanan and Gordon Tullock in their co-authored book *Calculus of Consent* (Ann Arbor: University of Michigan Press, 1962) and later works seem to be trying to ground their social contract theory in the libertarian's ideal of liberty alone.

38. In what follows, I shall piece together an account drawing mainly upon the articles Rawls has published since *A Theory of Justice*. In particular, see "Reply to Alexander and Musgrave," *Quarterly Journal of Economics*, vol. 88 (1974); "A Kantian Conception of Equality," *Cambridge Review* (1975); "Fairness to Goodness," *Philosophical Review*, vol. 84 (1975); "Kantian Constructivism in Moral Theory," *The Journal of Philosophy*, vol. 57 (1980); "Social Unity and Primary Goods," Amartya Sen and Bernard Williams, eds., *Utilitarianism and Beyond* (Cambridge: Cambridge University Press, 1982).

39. Rawls, "Kantian Constructivism in Moral Theory," p. 523 (my emphasis).

40. See John Rawls, *A Theory of Justice* (Cambridge: Harvard University Press, 1971), pp. 150-161. See also "Some Reasons for the Maximin Criterion," *American Economic Review*, vol. 64 (1974); "A Kantian Conception of Equality."

41. For the utilitarian view, see John C. Harsanyi, *Essays on Ethics, Social Behavior and Scientific Explanation* (Boston: Reidel Publishing Co., 1976), Chapters IV, V; "Morality and the Theory of Rational Behavior," *Social Research*, vol. 44 (1977); Dennis C. Mueller, Robert Tollison and Thomas Willett, "The Utilitarian Contract," *Theory and Decision* (1974). For the compromise view, see my "Justice as Desert," *Social Theory and Practice*, vol. 3 (1974); *The Demands of Justice* (Notre Dame: University of Notre Dame Press, 1980), Chapter 2; and "The Welfare Rights of Distant Peoples and Future Generations: Moral Side-Constraints on Social Policy," *Social Theory and Practice*, vol. 10 (1981). See also David Gauthier, "Justice and Natural Endowment," *Social Theory and Practice*, vol. 3 (1974); Michael Gardiner, "Rawls on the Maximin Rule and Distributive Justice," *Philosophical Studies*, vol. 28 (1975).

42. Sterba, *The Demands of Justice*, especially Chapter 2.

43. Rawls, "Kantian Conception of Equality," pp. 98-99.

44. For the argument, see my article "How Best to Critique Utilitarianism," Robert Almeder, ed., *Praxis and Reason* (Washington, DC: University Press of America, 1982). For the plausibility of interpreting primary goods in terms of utility see Jan Narveson, "Rawls and Utilitarianism," Harlan Miller and William Williams, eds., *The Limits of Utilitarianism* (Minneapolis: University of Minnesota Press, 1982), pp. 139-140.

45. Kenneth Arrow, "Some Ordinalist-Utilitarian Notes on Rawls's Theory of Justice," *The Journal of Philosophy*, vol. 50 (1973), pp. 245-263.

46. There will, however, be a need to revise somewhat the standard axioms of utility theory. See Amos Tversky, "A Critique of Expected Utility Theory: Descriptive and Normative Considerations," *Erkenntnis*, vol. 13 (1975), pp. 163-173.

47. For an earlier discussion of this point, see my "In Defense of Rawls Against Arrow and Nozick," *Philosophia*, Special Issue, vol. 7 (1978), pp. 293-303.

48. See *Old Age Insurance*, submitted to the Joint Economic Committee of the Congress of the United States in December 1967, p. 186, and *Statistical Abstracts of the United States for 1979*, p. 434.

49. See Sar Levitan, *Programs in Aid of the Poor* (Baltimore: Johns Hopkins University Press, 1976), pp. 2-4; David Gordon, "Trends in Poverty," David Gordon, ed., *Problems in Political Economy: An Urban Perspective* (Lexington, MA: C. Heath, 1971), pp. 297-298; Arthur Simon, *Bread for the World* (New York: Paulist Press, 1975), Chapter 8.

50. S. Benn and R.S. Peters, *The Principles of Political Thought* (New York: The Free Press, 1959), p. 167.

51. *Statistical Abstracts for 1985*, p. 446.

52. See Bernard Gendron, *Technology and the Human Condition* (New York: St. Martin's Press, 1977), pp. 222-227.

53. Alasdair MacIntyre, *After Virtue* (Notre Dame: University of Notre Dame Press, 1981).

54. Alvin Goldman, *A Theory of Human Action* (Englewood Cliffs: Prentice–Hall, 1970), pp. 208-215; William Frankena, "Obligation and Ability," Max Black, ed., *Philosophical Analysis* (Ithaca: Cornell University Press, 1950), pp. 157-175.
Judging from some recent discussions of moral dilemmas by Bernard Williams and Ruth Marcus, one might think that the "ought implies can" principle would only be useful for illustrating moral conflicts rather than resolving them. See Bernard Williams, *Problem of the Self* (Cambridge: Cambridge University Press, 1973), Chapters 11 and 12; Ruth Marcus, "Moral Dilemmas and Consistency," *The Journal of Philosophy*, vol. 57 (1980), pp. 121-136. See also Terrance C. McConnell, "Moral Dilemmas and Consistency in Ethics," *Canadian Journal of Philosophy*, vol. 8 (1978), pp. 269-287. But this is only true if one interprets the "can" in the principle to exclude only "what a person lacks the power to do." If one interprets the "can" to exclude in addition "what would involve so great a sacrifice that it would be unreasonable to ask the person to do it," then the principle can be used to resolve moral conflicts as well as state them. Nor would libertarians object to this broader interpretation of the "ought implies can" principle since they do not ground their claim to liberty on the existence of irresolvable moral conflicts, in which people could be morally required to do what it is unreasonable for them to do.

55. See my paper, "Is There a Rationale for Punishment?" *The American Journal of Jurisprudence*, vol. 29 (1984).

56. Obviously, the employment opportunities and voluntary welfare assistance offered to the poor must be honorable and supportive of self-respect. To do otherwise would be to offer the poor the chance to meet some of their basic needs at the cost of denying some their other basic needs.

57. The poor cannot, however, give up the liberty to which their children are entitled.

58. See John Hospers, "The Libertarian Manifesto," James P. Sterba, ed., *Morality in Practice* (Belmont: Wadsworth Publishing Co., 1983), especially p. 26.

59. Sometimes advocates of libertarianism inconsistently contend that the duty to help others is supererogatory but that a majority of a society could justifiably enforce such a duty on everyone. See Theodore Benditt, "The Demands of Justice," Diana Meyers and Kenneth Kipnis, eds., *Economic Justice* (Totowa, NJ: Rowman and Allanheld, 1985).

60. Sometimes advocates of libertarianism focus on the coordination problems that arise in welfare states concerning the provision of welfare and ignore the far more serious coordination problems that would arise in a nightwatchman state. See Burton Leiser, "Vagrancy, Loitering and Economic Justice," Meyers and Kipnis, eds., *Economic Justice*.

61. It is true, of course, that if the rich could retain the resources that are used in a welfare liberal state for meeting the basic needs of the poor, they would have the option of using those resources to increase employment opportunities beyond what obtains in any given welfare state, but this particular way of increasing employment opportunities would be counterproductive with respect to meeting basic needs overall, and particularly counterproductive with respect to meeting the basic needs of those who cannot work.

62. For the argument, see my "The Welfare Rights of Distant Peoples and Future Generations: Moral Side-Constraints on Social Policy."

63. *ibid.*

64. Bob Bergland, "Attacking the Problem of World Hunger," *The National Forum*, vol. 69 (1979), p. 4.

65. Diana Manning, *Society and Food* (Sevenoaks, KY: Butterworths, 1977), p. 12; Arthur Simon, *Bread for the World*, p. 14.

66. Roger Revelle, "Food and Population," *Scientific American*, vol. 231 (September 1974), p. 168.

67. Lester Brown, "Population, Cropland and Food Prices," *The National Forum*, vol. 69 (1979), pp. 11-17.

68. Janet Besecker and Phil Elder, "Lifeboat Ethics: A Reply to Hardin," William R. Burch, Jr., ed., *Readings in Ecology, Energy and Human Society: Contemporary Perspectives* (New York: Harper and Row, 1977), p. 229.

69. There definitely are numerous possibilities for utilizing more and more efficient means of satisfying people's basic needs in developed societies. For example, the American food industry manufactured for the U.S. Agriculture Department CSM, a product made of corn, soy and dried milk, which supplied all the necessary nutrients and 70 percent of minimum calorie intake for children.

70. Joel Feinberg, "Is There a Right to be Born?" James Rachels, ed., *Understanding Moral Philosophy* (Belmont: Dickinson Publishing Co., 1976), p. 354.

71. Jan Narveson, "Moral Problems of Population," *Monist*, vol. 57 (1973), p. 68.

72. *ibid.*, pp. 62-72.

73. Trudy Govier, "What Should We Do About Future People?" *American Philosophical Quarterly*, vol. 12 (1979), pp. 105-113.

74. For the practical implications with respect to contraception and the choice to have children, see my "Abortion, Distant Peoples and Future Generations," *The Journal of Philosophy*, vol. 50 (1980), pp. 424-440.

75. Federal Reserve Board, "Survey of Consumer Finances, 1983: A Second Report," reprinted from the *Federal Reserve Bulletin* (Washington, DC, December 1984), pp. 857-868; Richard Parker, *The Myth of the Middle Class* (New York: Harper and Row, 1972), p. 212.

76. Karl Marx, *Capital*, vol. 1 (New York: International Publishers, 1967), p. 715.

77. Karl Marx and Friedrich Engels, *Communist Manifesto* (Chicago: Charles Kerr & Co., 1888), p. 47.

78. Clark and Gintis, "Rawlsian Justice," pp. 312-313.

79. For considerations that favor worker control, see Harry Braveman, *Labor and Monopoly Capitalism*; Carole Pateman, *Participation and Democratic Theory; Work in America*; Clark and Gintis, "Rawlsian Justice," pp. 302-325.

80. There may also be a need for some governmental control of the flow of investment to ensure that individuals as consumers would be able to satisfy their basic needs.

81. *Economic Pastoral*, p. 46.

Part 2

1. National Conference of Catholic Bishops, *Economic Justice for All: Catholic Social Teaching and the U.S. Economy* (Third Draft), *Origins*, vol. 16 (June 5, 1986), p. 43 [hereinafter referred to as the *Economic Pastoral*].

2. *ibid.*, p. 42, paragraph 82.

3. "In democratic countries these [civil and political] rights have been secured through a long and vigorous history of creating the institutions of constitutional government. In seeking to secure the full range of social and economic rights, a similar effort to shape new economic arrangements will be necessary." *Economic Pastoral*, p. 42, paragraph 81. Also, the Catholic Bishops state in their second draft that "these economic rights should be granted a status in the cultural and legal traditions of this nation analogous to that held by the civil and political rights to freedom of religion, speech and assembly." "Second Draft of the U.S. Bishops' Pastoral Letter on Catholic Social Teaching and the U.S. Economy," *Origins*, vol. 15, no. 17 (October 10, 1985), p. 267, paragraph 85.

4. *Economic Pastoral*, p. 45, paragraph 120.

5. *ibid.*, p. 42, paragraph 80.

6. *ibid.*, p. 36, paragraph 27.

7. This essay does not attempt to evaluate the bishops' biblical and religious perspective.

8. The use of the words *moral vision* should in no way be taken as implying that this essay is only concerned with a common cultural consensus. Rather, these words are used to refer to a moral theory which is attempting to provide genuine knowledge or insight.

9. *Economic Pastoral*, p. 35, paragraph 19.

10. The extremely important issue of justifying the existence of moral knowledge is beyond the scope of this essay, but it is hoped that the sketch of what the author regards as the appropriate view of human dignity will indicate how this issue could be addressed. The reader interested in this issue should see the following by Douglas B. Rasmussen: "Essentialism, Values, and Rights," Tibor R. Machan, ed., *The Libertarian Reader* (Totowa, NJ: Rowman and Littlefield, 1982), pp. 37-52; "A Groundwork for Rights: Man's Natural End," *The Journal of Libertarian Studies*, vol. 4 (Winter 1980), pp. 65-76; "The Open-Question Argument and the Issue of Conceivability," *Proceedings of the American Catholic Philosophical Association*, vol. 56 (1982), pp. 162-172; and with Douglas J. Den Uyl, "In Defense of Natural End Ethics: A Rejoinder to O'Neil and Osterfeld," *The Journal of Libertarian Studies*, vol. 7 (Spring 1983), pp. 115-125. Also, see Eric Mack, "How to Derive Libertarian Rights," Jeffrey Paul, ed., *Reading Nozick* (Totowa, NJ: Rowman and Littlefield, 1981), pp. 286-302; Tibor R. Machan, *Human Rights and Human Liberties* (Chicago: Nelson-Hall, 1975).

11. Strictly speaking, if morality is the guide to human action and if there is no moral knowledge—if no course of action is better than any other—there would be no more reason *not* to invoke a moral vision than to invoke a moral vision, or vice versa. There would, of course, be no point to doing anything; for there would be, as Henry B. Veatch has noted, "no possible way in which the denial of all standards of better and worse [could] itself be transformed into a kind of standard of better and worse." *Rational Man* (Bloomington, IN: Indiana University Press, 1962), p. 45.

12. *Economic Pastoral*, p. 36, paragraph 28 (emphasis in original). David Hollenbach, S.J. notes: "Human dignity is...more fundamental than any specific human right. It is the source of all moral principles, not a moral principle itself." *Claims In Conflict* (New York: Paulist Press, 1979), p. 90.

13. *Economic Pastoral*, p. 40, paragraph 61. In *Claims In Conflict*, Hollenbach describes human dignity as an "ontological characteristic of every person," which is "nearly empty of meaning" without reference to "particular needs, actions, and relationships" (p. 90). He further describes human dignity as "a transcendental characteristic of persons...not identical with the fulfillment of any need, with the freedom for any particular type of action or with the attainment

of any specific kind of relationship" (p. 91). Yet, except for discussions of the historical development of the notion of human dignity in Roman Catholic teaching and its theological foundation
(*imago Dei*), there is very little helpful discussion in this otherwise most helpful book of what it is
about human nature that justifies the claim that human beings *have* dignity—that human
dignity is an ontological characteristic of every person.

14. The Catholic Bishops do not, however, regard human flourishing or fulfillment as the final
purpose or end but only the natural end; for they believe that man has a supernatural end. "The
fulfillment of human needs...is not the final purpose of the creation of the human person. We
have been created to share in the divine life that goes far beyond our human capabilities and
before which we must in all humility stand in awe." *Economic Pastoral*, p. 67, paragraph 360.
The natural and supernatural ends are not, however, regarded as conflicting.

15. Gilbert Harman accuses this approach to morality of leading to both relativism and
consequentialism. See his article, "Human Flourishing, Ethics, and Liberty," *Philosophy &
Public Affairs*, vol. 12 (Fall 1983), pp. 307-322. Yet, see Tibor Machan's response to Harman,
"Harman's 'Refutation' of the Flourishing Ethics," *The Thomist*, vol. 49 (July 1985), pp.
387-391, as well as David Norton's response, "Is 'Flourishing' A True Alternative Ethics?"
Reason Papers, no. 10 (Spring 1985), pp. 101-105. Also, John M. Cooper argues that it is
incorrect to regard human flourishing as an end which makes all other ends only valuable as a
means to it and thus that a human flourishing ethic does not necessarily lead to consequentialism. See his *Reason and Human Good in Aristotle* (Cambridge, MA and London:
Harvard University Press, 1975), pp. 87-88 and Chapter Two.

16. Some Catholic thinkers might take exception to this description and insist that only God
can be an end-in-himself. They might claim that human beings can be ends-in-themselves only
in the sense that they are created in the image of God. Either way, human dignity is something
that requires that persons not be used for projects other than the ones they naturally have.

Also, it is certainly possible to hold that people can be ends-in-themselves without accepting
that human flourishing is the natural end for man, as Kant, for example, does. Of course, it is
questionable whether Kant can sustain this claim without recourse to some grounding of the
"ought" in an "is"; for in virtue of what is an individual an end-in-himself? According to an ethic
of human flourishing, people are actual ends-in-themselves if, and only if, they conduct themselves in ways that will allow them to actualize their individuative and generic potentialities, i.e.,
to attain their natural end. Being an actual end-in-oneself is thus a state that must be earned; but
every person is a potential end-in-himself simply in virtue of being a living creature whose
potentialities are actualized through his own self-directed behavior. While actually being an end-
in-oneself is the primary ethical concern, protecting the status of persons as potential ends-in-
themselves is the primary social concern.

17. *Economic Pastoral*, p. 40, paragraph 64.

18. *ibid.*, p. 41, paragraph 71.

19. *ibid.*, p. 40, paragraph 65.

20. This is the first precept of the natural law according to St. Thomas Aquinas. It is based on
the belief that the natural end of a thing is the good at which it aims. Regarding human beings,
this means that "if a man is to become a mature and responsible adult, there are certain things he
must do, certain ways he must go about it; if he neglects these, it will mean that his natural end
will not be achieved and his life will be, if not a downright failure, than at least not what it might
have been or ought to have been." Henry B. Veatch, *For An Ontology of Morals* (Evanston, IL:
Northwestern University Press, 1971), p. 123. See pp. 106-123 of this work for an excellent
explanation and defense of this belief.

21. *Economic Pastoral*, p. 40, paragraph 69.

22. *ibid.*, p. 41, paragraph 71.

23. *ibid.*, p. 40, paragraph 70.

24. See Josef Pieper, *The Four Cardinal Virtues* (Notre Dame, IN: University of Notre Dame Press, 1980), pp. 56-57 for this distinction. Though the Catholic Bishops speak of "justice" and "basic justice," they never discuss what the relationship between the two concepts is.

25. *Economic Pastoral*, p. 42, paragraph 79.

26. *ibid.*, p. 41, paragraph 78.

27. *ibid.*, p. 42, paragraph 84 (emphasis in original).

28. Pope John XXIII, *Pacem in Terris*, paragraph 11, David J. O'Brien and Thomas A. Shannon, eds., *Renewing the Earth: Catholic Documents on Peace, Justice, and Liberation* (Garden City, NY: Doubleday, 1977), p. 126.

29. *Economic Pastoral*, p. 45, paragraph 119 (emphasis added).

30. *ibid.*, p. 40, paragraph 62.

31. The Catholic Bishops offer virtually no philosophical justification or defense of the duties they claim each and every human being has. Further, it seems that they treat all human virtues, except concern for the poor, on an equal level and do not explain why concern for the poor, as opposed to some other human virtue, should be given special priority.

32. Joel Feinberg has noted that etymologically the word *duty* was associated with the payments of debts to creditors and the keeping of contracts. *Social Philosophy* (Englewood Cliffs, NJ: Prentice-Hall, 1973), p. 63.

33. Consider this argument: "I ought to treat others justly," therefore, "Others have a right to be treated justly by me." The problem here is the ambiguity of the term "justice." If it refers to any obligation or duty I owe another, then the conclusion does not follow. The difficulty, of course, is specifying that sense of "justice" which would allow this argument to work. Yet, even then, it does not seem that the notion of "a right" is adequately captured. A right is a deeper moral concept than either the concepts of justice or duty. Though certainly not unrelated to justice or duty, it seems to flow from my own principled commitment to human flourishing more than from a duty others owe to me.

34. John Rawls, *A Theory of Justice* (Cambridge, MA: Harvard University Press, 1971); Alan Gewirth, *Reason and Morality* (Chicago: University of Chicago Press, 1978); A.I. Melden, *Persons and Rights* (Berkeley, CA: University of California Press, 1977); Ronald Dworkin, *Taking Rights Seriously* (Cambridge, MA: Harvard University Press, 1977).

35. The rights discussed here are often called "claim-rights" and are differentiated from other conceptions of rights by the fact that they are necessarily linked with the duties of other people.

36. See Eric Mack's "Introduction" and Tibor R. Machan's "Moral Myths and Basic Positive Rights," Eric Mack, ed., *Tulane Studies in Philosophy: Positive and Negative Duties*, vol. 23 (1985). Also, see John Hospers, *Human Conduct*, 2nd ed. (New York: Harcourt Brace Jovanovich, 1982), pp. 245-246.

37. *Economic Pastoral*, pp. 42-43, paragraph 89 (emphasis in original).

38. Pope Paul VI, *Populorum Progressio*, paragraph 23, O'Brien and Shannon, eds., *Renewing the Earth*, p. 320.

39. *Economic Pastoral*, p. 42, paragraph 80.

40. Being compelled to perform is as much an infringement of the freedom of speech as being prohibited from performing. Further, the singers would be prohibited from performing elsewhere while they performed at this compulsory concert.

41. See Douglas B. Rasmussen, "Conceptions of the Common Good and the Natural Right to Liberty," Rocco Porreco, ed., *The Georgetown Symposium On Ethics: Essays in Honor of Henry Babcock Veatch* (Lanham, NY, and London: University Press of America, 1984), pp. 185-193.

42. See Machan, *Human Rights and Human Liberties*, and Mack, "How to Derive Libertarian Rights." Yet, one should also see and read carefully Ayn Rand, *The Virtue of Selfishness* (New York: The New American Library, 1964), and *Capitalism: The Unknown Ideal* (New York: The New American Library, 1967), especially the essay "Man's Rights" which appears in both works. Finally, for appraisals, both pro and con, on Rand's philosophical efforts, see Douglas J. Den Uyl and Douglas B. Rasmussen, eds., *The Philosophic Thought of Ayn Rand* (Urbana and Chicago: University of Illinois Press, 1984).

43. Eric Mack, "How to Derive Libertarian Rights," p. 290 (some emphasis added).

44. This paragraph, as well as many other views expressed in this essay, are explored (and defended) in greater detail in a book I am coauthoring with Douglas J. Den Uyl. The book is tentatively titled *Towards Liberty: A Neo-Aristotelian Approach to Natural Rights.*

45. Immanuel Kant, *Fundamental Principles of the Metaphysic of Morals*, trans. Thomas K. Abbott (Chicago: Henry Regnery, 1949), section 2, p. 53.

46. See Alasdair MacIntyre, *After Virtue* (Notre Dame, IN: University of Notre Dame Press, 1981), pp. 44-45.

47. Commonsensically, we would say of this person that "he has no self-respect." Metaphysically, we would say that he denies that he has the potentiality to be an end-in-himself.

48. Mack, "How to Derive Libertarian Rights," p. 291.

49. More precisely, the error here is in treating "moral good" as if it existed apart from the choices and actions of human beings.

50. There may, of course, be circumstances in which it is better that others be in charge of one's life, e.g., when one undergoes surgery, but this situation would not be a morally good one unless the choice to undergo surgery was one's own. There are also situations in which someone is too young, old, sick, or injured to make such decisions, but these cases do not refute the claim that it is always better for a human being to be self-directed than not to be self-directed. Rather, they merely show that there are situations in which this claim would have no point because of the principle that ought implies can. Yet, even in these situations the importance of autonomy is stressed; for in cases in which it is possible to know the choices of the incapacitated party (or reasonably project what the incapacitated party would choose), we try to honor those choices.

51. Ayn Rand, "Man's Rights," *Capitalism: The Unknown Ideal*, p. 322.

52. John Hospers, *Human Conduct*, p. 254.

53. Tibor R. Machan, "Moral Myths and Basic Positive Rights," p. 39. Also, see Tibor R. Machan, "Individualism and the Problem of Political Authority," *The Monist*, vol. 66 (October 1983), pp. 500-516, and "Dissolving the Public Goods Problem: Financing Government Without Coercive Measures," *The Libertarian Reader*, pp. 201-208.

54. To those familiar with Leo Strauss's work, *Natural Right and History*, it should be apparent that the view of negative human rights presented in the previous section is based on more than natural "powers" possessed by human beings in some state of nature; rather, the rights are based on a certain understanding of a human being's *telos*. Whether Strauss was correct in

claiming that Locke's argument for negative natural rights was based on nothing more than the claim that human beings are free and equal by nature and thus (?) ought to be free and equal, or whether Locke's account of nature was not as radically amoral as Hobbes presents nature to be, there is no reason to assume that negative natural rights cannot be grounded in a natural-end ethics. See Eric Mack, "Locke's Arguments for Natural Rights," *Southwestern Journal of Philosophy*, vol. 10 (Spring 1980), pp. 51-60, for an account of Locke that takes issue with Strauss's view of Locke. Also, see Henry B. Veatch, *Human Rights: Fact or Fancy?* (Baton Rouge and London: Louisiana State University Press, 1985), for an argument for negative natural rights which appeals to a human being's *telos*. Veatch holds that these rights are inalienable. Yet, he does not hold that they are absolute.

55. Henry B. Veatch, *Human Rights: Fact or Fancy?*, p. 85 (emphasis added).

56. Tibor R. Machan, *Human Rights and Human Liberties*, p. 119.

57. Ayn Rand, *Atlas Shrugged* (New York: Random House, 1957), p. 1061 (some emphasis added).

58. From the foregoing conception of human flourishing, it can be observed that two types of moral considerations can be used to morally evaluate a person's actions. As Eric Mack has noted: "There is the consideration of whether B employs his actions in accord with their proper end and there is the consideration of whether B prevents A's activity, capacities, and so on from being employed in accord with their proper end. If B's action is unjustified on the basis of the latter consideration, it is unjustified on the basis of the character of his treatment of A and not on the basis of the effectiveness with which his (proper) goals are pursued. Such action would be deontically unjustified and A has a claim against such action in virtue of his being a moral end-in-himself. A similar claim can be made on behalf of (at least) each human person. And for each of them this claim constitutes a natural (non-special) human right." See Eric Mack, "How to Derive Libertarian Rights," p. 291. Also, see Douglas J. Den Uyl and Douglas B. Rasmussen, "Nozick on the Randian Argument," Jeffrey Paul, ed., *Reading Nozick* (Totowa, NJ: Rowman and Littlefield, 1981), pp. 250-259. This argument also assumes that practical reasoning exists, i.e., that rational desires are possible, and that human beings are not "slaves to their passions" and thus can act on the basis of moral principles. See Norman O. Dahl, *Practical Reason, Aristotle, and Weakness of the Will* (Minneapolis, MN: University of Minnesota Press, 1984), for an excellent discussion and defense of these assumptions.

59. Robert Nozick, *Anarchy, State, and Utopia* (New York: Basic Books, 1974), p. 57. The notion of "moral space" is a crucial concept in the theory of negative rights presented here, but it cannot be adequately discussed within the confines of this essay.

60. Developing a legal system for the implementation of a system of rights is a large and complicated task. See J.C. Smith, "The Processes of Adjudication and Regulation: A Comparison," Tibor R. Machan and M. Bruce Johnson, eds., *Rights and Regulation* (Cambridge, MA: Ballinger, 1983), pp. 71-96.

61. If rights are to have the fundamental role of determining what matters of morality are to be matters of law, and if rights are to be moral principles applicable to human social and political life which ought to be respected regardless of the consequences, then it is the absoluteness of rights that gives rights the particular normative force they have. As John Hospers has noted, "What value is a right if others can be justified in violating it? It is the absoluteness of rights that makes us secure in claiming them, as we would not be if they were only prima facie." *Human Conduct*, p. 254. Human rights simply cannot have the fundamental role assigned to them in a theory of justice if they are *all* prima facie. "If every right can be over-ruled by another right, and if having a fundamental place in a scheme of justice means that whatever occupies that place

serves as the court of last resort in settling questions of justice, then natural rights cannot serve the purpose for which they have been introduced, namely to enable us to identify justice, distinguish it from injustice, and act accordingly in a social context....[This] characterization of the items that have a fundamental place in our scheme of justice would render them systematically *ad hoc* in that each case where one will stop the process of over-ruling cannot have systematic determination." Tibor R. Machan, "Prima Facie Versus Natural (Human) Rights," *The Journal of Value Inquiry*, vol. 10 (1976), p 127.

62. Christopher W. Morris, "Natural Rights And Public Goods," Thomas Attig, Donald Callen, and John Gray, eds., *The Restraint of Liberty: Bowling Green Studies in Applied Philosophy*, vol. 7 (Bowling Green, OH: Bowling Green State University, 1985), p. 115, n. 5.

63. John Hospers, *Human Conduct*, p. 269. Further, the Catholic Bishops seem to avoid this dilemma by recognizing that if there were an absolute scarcity of resources which made it impossible to fulfill everyone's basic needs, then the obligation to fulfill these needs would no longer be in force. Yet, the Catholic Bishops do not discuss in what sense, if any, they would consider economic rights to be "absolute" or what they mean by "rights." They do nonetheless maintain that relief of the poor should come "not merely out of our superfluous goods," and since no absolute scarcity exists in the United States today, the Catholic Bishops would have the resources of every citizen of the United States reduced to the minimum level necessary for human life if that was what was required to make sure others have sufficient resources necessary to meet their basic needs. *Economic Pastoral*, pp. 40-41, paragraph 70.

64. Eric Mack has noted that the key to seeing what is morally wrong with threats of coercion, e.g., "your money or your dissertation manuscript," is that the person who makes the threat does not have the right to the item offered in "exchange." See "Individualism, Rights, and the Open Society," Tibor R. Machan, ed., *The Libertarian Reader*, pp. 13-14.

65. See Ayn Rand, "The Ethics of Emergencies," *The Virtue of Selfishness*, pp. 43-49; Tibor R. Machan, "Human Rights: Some Points of Clarification," *The Journal of Critical Analysis* (July/October 1973), pp. 30-39; and Eric Mack, "Individualism, Rights, and the Open Society," pp. 3-15. Further, it should be noted that "absolute" does not necessarily mean unconditional; for these rights are not self-evident moral truths. They are justified by reference to man's natural end.

66. Ayn Rand, "Requiem For Man," *Capitalism: The Unknown Ideal*, p. 299.

67. *Economic Pastoral*, p. 45, paragraph 121.

68. See Bernard Bailyn, *The Ideological Origins of the American Revolution* (Cambridge, MA: Belknap Press of Harvard University Press, 1967); and Bernard H. Siegan, *Economic Liberties and the Constitution* (Chicago and London: University of Chicago Press, 1980).

69. Henry B. Veatch, *Human Rights: Fact or Fancy?*, p. 205 (some emphasis added).

70. *Economic Pastoral*, p. 41, paragraph 78.

71. David Hollenbach, S.J., *Claims In Conflict*, p. 97.

72. David Hollenbach states: "Catholic rights theory is far removed from individualist or libertarian social philosophy. The theory presented in the encyclicals is personalist, not individualist." *Claims In Conflict*, p. 97. This distinction mirrors Jacques Maritain's distinction between "personality" which characterizes the spiritual side of human nature and "individuality" which characterizes the material side of human nature in his now classic *The Person and the Common Good* (South Bend, IN: University of Notre Dame Press, 1966). Though this distinction cannot be adequately considered here, it should at least be observed that, despite Maritain's claim to the contrary, his construal of the matter and form of a human being constitutes an unfortunate bifurcation of human nature. "Man's unified nature demands that care be taken in describing his

mode of being. Our so called 'material' side is every bit as constitutive of what we are as the 'spiritual' side. It is thus more than misleading to attribute such processes as knowing and loving to one side—'personality'—while leaving the other side—'individuality'—to do no more than locate us in space." Douglas J. Den Uyl and Douglas B. Rasmussen, "Liberty and the Common Good," (unpublished manuscript), p. 7. This essay constitutes chapter four of the book manuscript tentatively titled, *Towards Liberty: A Neo-Aristotelian Approach to Natural Rights.*

73. David Hollenbach, S.J., *Claims In Conflict*, p. 166.

74. Peiper, *The Four Cardinal Virtues*, p. 98.

75. D.J. Allan, "Individual and State in the *Ethics* and *Politics*," *Entriens Sur l'Antiquite Classique* (1965), pp. 55-95.

76. I owe this distinction to Douglas J. Den Uyl.

77. This is not merely a problem of size. Human beings are very different. Though alike in possessing the capacity to reason and choose, their humanity is manifested in numerous ways. Each person's life plan is so different that it is hard to see how there could be a single determinate end everyone could aim to achieve. Moreover, everyone striving to achieve one single end does not seem something desirable: for self-actualization is a process that is accomplished in many ways. Further, to achieve sufficient universality regarding a single end would require creating a society along Orwellian lines, and even then it would fail. A human group is a *noetic* and *moral* entity, and these are the very things that state coercion would destroy.

78. Ayn Rand, "From My 'Future File'," *Ayn Rand Letter 3* (September 23, 1974), pp. 4-5. D.J. Allan has observed that Aristotle does not "credit the politician, in his capacity as lawgiver, with the power of manufacturing happiness or virtue, but represents him as *establishing the framework* within which happiness can be attained." "Individual and State in the *Ethics* and *Politics*," p. 66.

79. See comment on Maritain's conception of the common good in note 72.

80. Douglas J. Den Uyl, Letter to the Author, September 14, 1983.

81. There is undoubtedly more to be said about this complicated and vexing notion, not the least of which is a discussion of how a society based on negative human rights would deal with the problem of "public goods." See Tibor R. Machan, "Dissolving the Problem of Public Goods: Financing Government Without Coercive Measures," *The Libertarian Reader*, pp. 201-208.

82. *Economic Pastoral*, p. 46, paragraph 128.

83. In the first draft of the *Economic Pastoral*, the Catholic Bishops noted that their view of justice was in agreement with that of John Rawls regarding the "general conception of justice," according to which all basic social goods, including basic rights, are to be distributed equally unless unequal distribution of any or all of these goods is to the advantage of the least well-off members of society. All mention of Rawls is dropped in the second and third drafts, but it still seems possible to use a Rawlsian form of social contract theory to argue for the view of rights the Catholic Bishops endorse. Yet, see Douglas B. Rasmussen, "A Critique of Rawls' *Theory of Justice*," *The Personalist*, vol. 55 (Summer 1974), pp. 303-318, for a criticism of Rawlsian methodology, as well as his concept and conception of justice. Also, see Jeffrey Paul, "Substantive Social Contracts and the Basis for Political Authority," *The Monist*, vol. 66 (October 1983), p. 528, for an excellent general critique of contractarianism.

84. For the sake of the argument, assume that the politicians in question have outstanding moral character. The problem of providing some criteria for determining what should be made a matter of law remains.

85. *Economic Pastoral*, p. 45, paragraph 113.

86. As Rand has observed: "For every individual, a right is the moral sanction of a positive—of his freedom to act on his own judgment, for his own goals, by his *voluntary, uncoerced choice.* As to his neighbors, his rights impose no obligations on them except of a *negative* kind: to abstain from violating his rights." "Man's Rights," *Capitalism: The Unknown Ideal*, p. 322.

87. See Tibor R. Machan, "The Petty Tyranny of Government Regulation," Machan and Johnson, eds., *Rights and Regulation*, pp. 259-288.

88. Walter Williams, *The State Against Blacks* (New York: McGraw-Hill, 1982).

89. Bruce L. Gardner, *The Governing of Agriculture* (Lawrence, KS: University of Kansas Press, 1981), p. 130.

90. Charles Murray, *Losing Ground* (New York: Basic Books, 1984).

91. Murray's work has been accused of playing fast and loose with the data. Yet, see Murray's answer to his critics, "Have the Poor Been 'Losing Ground'?" *Political Science Quarterly*, vol. 100 (Fall 1985), pp. 427-445. Also, see Robert Royal, "Charles Murray & His Critics," *Catholicism In Crisis*, vol. 3 (July 1985), pp. 6-11; and George Gilder, "The Murray Imbroglio," *The American Spectator* (March 1985), pp. 15-18.

92. It should be remembered that a human group is a noetic and moral entity whose unity and existence results only from its members judging that common action is needed to attain an end and deciding to pursue that end. For an understanding of the corporation that is similar to this view of a human group, see Robert Hessen, *In Defense of the Corporation* (Stanford: Hoover Institution Press, 1979). Also, see Douglas J. Den Uyl, *The New Crusaders: The Corporate Social Responsibility Debate* (Bowling Green, OH: Social Philosophy and Policy Center, 1984).

93. F.A. Hayek, *The Road to Serfdom* (Chicago: University of Chicago Press, 1944), p. 89.

94. It should be added that in such a situation not only does having earned money indicate that one has been able to sell to others what they want, it also indicates the presence of many important moral virtues. This will be discussed shortly.

95. *Economic Pastoral*, p. 40, paragraph 70.

96. In this context, it is interesting to note that the claim that the world was originally "given to men in common" can be interpreted to mean that no one has a positive natural right to any specific piece of property. Before one acquires this right through thought and labor, no person has any more of a natural right to any natural object than any other. John Locke's claim that one acquires a right to a natural object by mixing his labor with it can be understood as an alternative to the views of Grotius and Pufendorf, who claimed that men had rights of a positive sort to natural objects.

97. Most of this paragraph is taken, with certain modifications, from Douglas B. Rasmussen, "Ethics and the Free Market," *Listening*, vol. 17 (Winter 1982), p. 84.

98. Douglas J. Den Uyl, "Freedom and Virtue Revisited," (forthcoming in a book of essays in honor of Murray N. Rothbard), p. 8.

99. The author wishes to thank John Ahrens, Caroline R. Bottone, and John S. Bonnici for their assistance.

Part 3

1. There is a dissimilarity in this respect between the U.S. Catholic Bishops' Pastoral Letter on War and Peace (*The Challenge of Peace*, Washington, DC: U.S. Catholic Conference, 1983) and the *Pastoral Letter on the U.S. Economy*. The earlier letter contains a quite respectable philosophical argument for its conclusions. Although the reasons for this difference are not entirely clear to me, it is interesting to note that the same difference shows up in the writings of Bryan Hehir and David Hollenbach, each of whom had an important role in the composition of the philosophical section of their respective letters. Bryan Hehir's writings are both philosophically and theologically based, whereas David Hollenbach's writings, especially his writings on political economy, are primarily theologically based.

2. For example, see Paul Taylor, *Principles of Ethics* (Belmont: Dickenson Publishing Co., 1975), pp. 26-29.

3. For example, see John Finnis, *Fundamentals of Ethics* (Washington, DC: Georgetown University Press, 1983), especially Chapter 5.

4. This is not to say, however, that the particular set of negative rights Rasmussen defends would emerge from such a foundation.

5. Of course, the main problem with such an account is that it will simply beg the question against opponents.

6. See Eric Mack, "Individualism, Rights and the Open Society," Tibor Michan, ed., *The Libertarian Alternative* (Chicago: Nelson-Hall, 1977), pp. 21-37, and "How to Derive Libertarian Rights," Jeffrey Paul, ed., *Reading Nozick* (Totowa, NJ: Rowman and Littlefield, 1981), pp. 286-302; Tibor Machan, *Human Rights and Human Liberties* (Chicago: Nelson-Hall, 1975).

7. *ibid*. See also Tibor Machan, "Recent Work on Ethical Egoism," *American Philosophical Quarterly*, vol. 16 (1979), pp. 1-15.

8. For example, see Mack, "Individualism, Rights and the Open Society," p. 29ff; Machan, *Human Rights and Human Liberties*, pp. 213-222; and Machan, "Human Rights: Some Points of Clarification," *Journal of Critical Analysis*, vol. 5 (1973), pp. 30-39.

9. Mack, "Individualism, Rights and the Open Society," p. 29.

10. Eric Mack, "Liberty and Justice"; a shorter version of this paper appeared under the same title in John Arthur and William Shaw, eds., *Justice and Economic Distribution* (Englewood Cliffs, NJ: Prentice-Hall, 1978), pp. 183-193.

11. In fact, while severe inequalities persist, there will be an inverse relationship between the amount of self-directedness or autonomy the rich are permitted to achieve and the amount of self-directedness or autonomy the poor are allowed to achieve.

12. These rights were not formulated explicitly in my contribution to this book, but they are clearly the rights that are implicit in my account.

13. As further evidence, notice that those libertarians who justify a minimal state do so on the grounds that such a state would arise from reasonable disagreements concerning the application of libertarian rights. They do not justify the minimal state on the grounds that it would be needed to keep in submission large numbers of people who could not come to see the reasonableness of libertarian rights.

Part 4

1. See John Gray, "Liberalism and the Choice of Liberties," Thomas Attig, Donald Callen, and John Gray, eds., *The Restraint of Liberty: Bowling Green Studies in Applied Philosophy*, vol. 7 (Bowling Green, OH: Bowling Green State University, 1985), pp. 1-25; Douglas B. Rasmussen, "Liberalism, Contractarianism, and the Choice of Liberties: A Response to Gray," pp. 26-36 in the same volume.

2. See the works of Tibor R. Machan and Eric Mack cited in my essay.

3. If Jones needed a kidney, would it be unreasonable for Smith to seek to prevent Jones from taking one of his surplus kidneys? See Fred Miller, Jr., "The Natural Right to Private Property," Tibor R. Machan, ed., *The Libertarian Reader* (Totowa, NJ: Rowman and Littlefield, 1982), pp. 275-287.

4. Ayn Rand, "Man's Rights," *Capitalism: The Unknown Ideal* (New York: The New American Library, 1967), pp. 322.

5. There can be situations in which social and political life is impossible and rights have no point—namely, when it is in principle impossible for all persons to pursue their well-being by the exercise of negative rights. As I noted in my essay, however, to admit that not all situations can be approached in terms of principles appropriate to social or political life implies nothing concerning the absoluteness of those principles. Rights are fundamental organizing principles of human communities whose function and purpose are tied to establishing a social and political context in which the highly individualized and self-directed character of human flourishing of all persons can be pursued. As long as this moral purpose can be attained, these negative rights apply and are absolute. A society governed by the negative rights to life, liberty, and property is one in which multiple means of seeking well-being that do not violate rights are available to persons. Such a society is, therefore, one that ought to be encouraged; for in such a society the possibility of there being situations in which it is impossible for persons to pursue their well-being by the exercise of negative rights is less likely to occur.

6. It is important to note that Sterba is not claiming that Smith has violated Jones's rights by *not* helping him. See James Sterba, "Recent Work On Alternative Conceptions of Justice," *The American Philosophical Quarterly*, vol. 23 (January 1986), p. 4 for his criticism of this approach. Also see Eric Mack, "Bad Samaritanism and the Causation of Harm," *Philosophy & Public Affairs*, vol. 9 (1980).